It's Not About the Banana

It's Not About the Banana

The 5-Step Method To Stop Living Other People's Lies and Start Living Your Truth

Tonya De'laine

Soul Shack Sisters

I dedicate this book to the Underdogs.

I see you
I understand you
I believe in you
I am you

And to my husband Jason, and my beautiful children, Gregory, Whitney, and Kendall.
Thank you for loving me when I could not love myself.

CONTENTS

CONTENTS

The Breakup to Wake Up

> ❝ The cave you fear to enter holds the treasure you seek. ❞
> ~ Joseph Campbell

Where the hell am I, and how did I get here? As I stood in a not-so-sterile shower at a mental hospital, this thought repeatedly played in my head. Seriously, is this my life? What is wrong with me? How did I allow this to happen?

I cried as I stood there, staring at a used nicotine patch (that wasn't mine, mind you) clogging the drain. I haven't cried in years! Well, at least not sober.

Yet there I was, bawling my eyes out while trying to keep quiet. I didn't want anyone to know I wasn't okay—like being in a mental hospital wasn't proof enough?

This is how my brain worked back then. I felt like I always had to play a role or be someone I wasn't to "feel" normal.

"Look how well that worked out for you, Tonya," I said out loud, to myself, while sobbing uncontrollably.

The tears continued pouring down my face as I felt defeated, worthless, and alone. I felt like I had finally hit ROCK BOTTOM—the kind where everything you once loved was gone, everything you worked so hard for had collapsed, and there was absolutely no one left to reach out to because you burned all the bridges (as well as the boats, dinghies, and lifejackets). That was me! Raw, extremely vulnerable, and 100% exposed. I had never felt such disgust for myself and the person I had become.

For the first time in my life, I could admit that I, Tonya, was an alcoholic! The one thing I said I would never be, I was. In accepting this Truth and surrendering to it with my entire being, I was finally able to Let Go. Let Go of the fight, Let Go of the lies, Let Go of trying to be someone I wasn't and permit myself to start becoming the person I was.

I embarked on a new journey of Self Discovery and my first real glimpse of a *"spiritual awakening"* that allowed me to write this book and share my story with you.

My life, up to that point, was a reflection of decisions and actions, followed by more decisions and actions, each with significant consequences. My life reflected what and who I allowed into it, and the lack of boundaries I failed to establish—the way I allowed others to treat me, or better yet, *mistreat me*, again and again. Little did I realize at the time that life *had* presented me with opportunities to advance; I just never stopped long enough to see or hear them.

As I slowly picked myself up off the shower floor, I promised myself I would do whatever it took to find myself again. I say "again" because there was once a time when I felt capable of something great. There was a time when I felt like I could do or be whatever I wanted. There was a time when I didn't feel this need to pretend to be someone I wasn't.

How did I become so disconnected from that version of myself?

When did I lose contact with her?

Where did she go?

Two weeks leading up to this pivotal shower moment, I was on a full-rage bender. Relapsing, I lost count of how many times; I was, without a doubt, out of control. I did things that I wouldn't think I was capable of. I missed my son's high school graduation. I was fired from my job. I was on the verge of being kicked out of my home because my now-husband couldn't stand to see the person I had become. I even went as far as taking an entire bottle of sleeping pills with the intent of not waking up.

It became clear *why* I ended up in that mental hospital, but what wasn't clear was *how* I became the type of person that belonged there.

After many manic attempts to reach my then-fiancé from the mental hospital, he finally picked up the phone.

"When are you coming to get me?" I cried. "They said I was free to leave hours ago."

"I'll be there soon," he replied and hung up.

I paced the floor of my room for what felt like an eternity before they told me my ride had finally arrived.

That car ride home was a heart-wrenching mixture of silent treatment and the most scolding anger I had ever received. As I sat there taking the verbal berating, I felt a peace come over me. Even though I knew I was heading up the steepest mountain I had ever climbed, I was determined to reach the summit. Little did I know that I was about to embark on a journey that would forever change my life and the lives of those around me. Within this peace, I felt a sense of calm and serenity.

Today I call this peace my Higher Power.

If you don't believe there is a God, don't let that stop you from reading this book. I get it; trust me, I do. I just ask that you be willing to have an open mind to the possibility that there is a higher frequency out there that is supporting you. You can call it whatever you like—Higher Power, Nature, the Universe, a Group of Deities, a power greater than you, whatever....

In fact, I believe that frequency and source energy led you to this book. I believe that everything happens for a purpose, and it's when we start to listen to what the Universe is trying to tell us that things begin to fall into place, and life becomes easier and more enjoyable.

That night I laid in bed replaying my entire life, trying to recall when it was that I lost Her. Thus began my journey back to my last known memory of feeling like I was unstoppable. I was six! *Holy Crap on a Cracker*, this was going to be a long road of recovery, but I knew I had to take it if I was going to keep this promise to myself. And looking back on it now, it was probably the first promise I ever kept to myself.

There I was in first grade, coloring a bat for Halloween. I was so proud of myself because while all the other kids took their time not to color outside the lines, I was coloring the entire page black. I was coloring outside the lines because I knew I would cut the bat out anyway, so why worry about the little details of staying within the lines? I never felt so alive, creative, and free to be Me.

"What are you doing?" a little boy sitting next to me asked. "You can't color outside the lines. You will get in trouble." At that moment, I froze with fear and panic. How could I have been so stupid? What if the teacher yells at me and I get in trouble? I had never felt so small. As I tried to explain my genius idea to my fellow six-year-old classmate, letting him know how creative I was, he called the teacher over to our table. While the teacher lectured me for not taking pride in my work, I lost myself in her every word. I remember trying to tell her what I was doing and that it would look just like all the other bats hanging in the window when I was done, but she didn't want to hear it. She gave me a new bat to color and tossed mine in the garbage.

What an experience for a young developing mind to have. What a message for a little girl to receive. Don't step outside the box we have created for you. Don't be different. Don't do you!

Now this example might sound exaggerated... but is it?

What is your earliest memory of when you were in "the zone," "doing you," and someone shammed you for it?

It doesn't have to be a significant event; it can be something as small as coloring outside the lines. We are slowly programmed to think and act a certain way in these little moments. To believe these lies (granted, they are innocent; but they are lies nonetheless), we start to accept them as our Truth. (I use Truth with a capital T as it relates to you.) These little lies add up throughout our lives, to the point that we don't know what our Truth is versus someone else's.

Now, I'm not saying you must go back to when you were six and re-live every moment after that; I am simply asking you to look at the first memory you have that changed you. That one simple shift in awareness will enliven your inner intelligence and be with you throughout this journey and beyond. It will help you navigate much of this self-transformation simply by acknowledging it.

What makes us act a certain way toward people, places, and things in our life?

It's our past experiences and memories.

The only part I played was in how I chose to show up; in how I repeated a vicious cycle of bad behavior and choices for most of my life. By not learning my lessons the first time.

I became so fearful of the lessons that I developed a coping mechanism of avoidance. I continued to believe *other people's lies* as *my* truth; I chose to continue to think those thoughts repeatedly, to the point that they became my identity.

When you live your life in survival mode, you may feel as if you are handling yourself well. But in reality, you are distancing yourself from who you really are, to the point that you are so far removed that you feel like a completely different person. The disconnect from my Truth found me standing in a dirty shower in a mental hospital.

This is why I wrote this book. I didn't want anyone else to have to go through what I did in order to reconnect to their Soul-Self. I knew I was given the gift of opportunity, and, God willing, I would take it.

The 5-Step Method will be revealed to you in each chapter based on my life. Because of this method that I developed during my journey, I finally realized the lies I was telling myself. I finally began to speak my Truth and was on my way to becoming the woman I was created to be.

I genuinely believe that we are all made for more, and it is in our life's journey that we acquire the skills and experiences needed to come full circle and share it with those we meet along the way.

When someone tells me I've come so far, I say, "No, *I was always this woman; I just finally caught up to her.*" The same is true for you. You are already the amazing, strong, talented, beautiful, and successful person you dream of becoming.

She is YOU, YOU are HER, and together we will reveal and heal her.

In this book, I will share my 5-Step Method to *uncover* the lies you've been living to *reveal* your *Truth*. This book is about how I peeled back the layers of my Soul's armor that I allowed to develop over 46 years to uncover my authentic self. I will share breakthroughs that helped me discover the revelations of my life's journey and purpose.

I hope my story helps you see similar patterns in your life that led you here today. My wish for you in reading this book is that you can uncover the lies you tell yourself or choose to believe as your truth; that you can identify your unsafe beliefs, face your fears, halt your excuses, and remove the self-doubt that prevents you from living your best, authentic self—your *Soul*-Self.

It's time to take back control of your life and face the limiting fears and beliefs you have allowed yourself to believe.

Let's peel back the layers of armor and discover the real meaning behind your fears, anxiety, doubt, guilt, and shame.

Raise YOUR voice, speak YOUR Truth, and once and for all, *unmute yourself!*

PART ONE

The 5-Step Method

> " Most of your healing journey will be about unlearning "
> the patterns of self-protection that once kept you safe.
>
> ~ Vironika Tugaleva

1

The Methodology Explained

The 5-Step Method

> " The journey of a thousand miles begins with one step. "
> ~ LAO TZU

First things first. Let's break down how this book was written and why. In **Part One**, you will learn about the 5-Step Method. This was designed with you in mind to easily access the steps you need to work on, and to help you quickly reference the questions and exercises as you need them. In **Part Two**, I share personal stories of when I uncovered the lies I had been living as my truth and how I recovered from Identity Sabotage using the Method.

As I share with you in the following chapters *HOW* the 5-Step Method works, I wanted to begin with *WHY* it works and what I discovered through my "spiritual awakening" that brought it to life. As I reflected on my life's journey up to this point, I had an *"aha"* moment. However, this epiphany wasn't a new concept for me, but a reinforced one. The actual "mind-blowing" moment occurred several years back when

I found myself in an argument with my now ex-husband over a banana, which is now the title of this book.

In this fight, I realized that most things we resist, argue, and fight over have nothing to do with the actual "thing" we decide to make it about. It's never about the thing.

It's not about the Banana!

Yes, I had a spiritual awakening over a banana. You see, the emotions we bring to the event that makes you feel and act a certain way actually have less to do with the present and more to do with the past. We want to believe it is about that thing or that person, when it's really about something deeper rooted within us just as much as it is with them (or it). We try to justify, defend, and prove our point, our beliefs, and our rightness instead of looking at the situation for what it really is.

Most times, whenever we feel cheated, used, mistreated, or misunderstood, it stems from a time when we felt unseen, unheard, and unloved. So we lash out, try to claim our point as valid, and ignore the Banana in the room. Or, in my case, use it as the deflector or distraction to avoid what the root cause of the symptoms we were both experiencing stemmed from.

I totally get why we avoid, run, deflect, or ignore the icky. It makes us uncomfortable. Who wants to feel uncomfortable? It's no wonder addiction is at an all-time high. We are overly medicated with substances that only cover up the symptoms instead of doing the work to find the *root* cause of the condition. Therefore, I started to develop a method that allowed me to address the "mind virus" step by step and take back my life.

For me, it's all about *Emotional Fitness*. When we can control our emotions, instead of allowing our emotions to control us, we begin to find clarity, gain a true sense of self-worth, stop apologizing for how we feel, and show up in the world. When we replace *"why is this happening to me"* with *"what is this trying to teach me,"* we slowly shift our mindset from a victim mentality to a victor mentality.

This is the power of the 5-Step Method.

PRESET (Finding Your Baseline)

PAUSE (Acknowledge and Identify the Emotional Response)

PEEL (Identify the Unsafe Belief)

REVEAL (Uncover the Root Cause of this Unsafe Belief, Acknowledge, and Let Go)

HEAL (Take your Power Back and Start Living Your Truth)

This is **WHY** it works; now it's time to find out **HOW**.

Before diving into the PAUSE, PEEL, REVEAL, and HEAL processes, we must first find our baseline emotionally. This is the first step. We all have one, and like you, they are as unique as your DNA. Every *SOUL* speaks and vibrates at a different frequency, and what rocks my boat may sink yours.

Therefore, it's essential to understand what makes you tick; sets you off; makes you want to run; or, worse yet, makes you want to hide and isolate yourself from the world.

Your baseline is one of calm and balance. It is where and when you feel peace, contentment, serenity, and acceptance of who you are and your life decisions. When challenged by people, places, and things in our life, it can push us away from our baseline. This is where our reptilian brain is activated—the fight, flight, freeze, or submit to SURVIVE, not THRIVE.

Remember, life is happening *for* us, not *to* us, so it is our job to identify when this is happening and what is really creating the frequency shift to occur.

Have you ever heard it said that too much of a good thing is a bad thing?

Yes, even those super good feelings can be a warning sign that may need our attention. I like to think of our emotions like the warning signs on our car's dashboard.

Engine overheating? Turn off the car or give it water.

Icy roads? Slow down.

Gaslight on? Time to pull over and fuel up.

Well, our body and its emotional dashboard are no different, and once we can establish its baseline, we will recognize sooner when it requires service or realignment.

Finding my baseline was something I became very passionate about, which eventually led to this guide/method that I am about to share with you.

I noticed that I was at the mercy of someone else's plan or emotional baggage at any given moment, and being an empath meant my car's dashboard lights were on constant alert. It was clear I had to find a better way to deal with these emotional rides. To make matters worse, I had now removed my only coping method—wine.

A few months into my sobriety, I was feeling pretty good. I was, without a doubt, on what they like to call in the recovery community "My Pink

Cloud." I felt terrific. I felt like nothing could stop me. I was determined to live my best life and go about my day with peace and purpose. Up to this point, I had completely shut out the external world.

My life was centered around 12-Step meetings and readings, followed by more meetings. When I wasn't working with my sponsor or on my Steps, I was either on the yoga mat, sitting in deep meditation, or working on my breathing.

But then LIFE got LIFIE.

The morning started like any other morning. I woke to my alarm, poured some coffee, and headed downstairs to do some yoga and meditation. The sun was shining and everything was going just right... until I had to interact with other humans. As I sat down to start my workday feeling recharged and aligned, my emails started pinging as the messages poured in.

When working in property management, there is never a dull day or a lack of challenging characters needing my immediate attention at any given moment. One problem after another was front and center, demanding to be solved. Soon the dog was pawing at me for food, the kids were calling for me to drop something off at their school that they had forgotten, and even my husband was texting me to see if we had milk in the fridge. *All at the same time!*

Before I realized it, my baseline was about to flatline as I felt all the feels.

I became short with my co-workers, yelled at the dog, and was ready to tell everyone to namaste away when I had this moment of clarity.

Remember, life is happening for *you, not* to *you.*

PAUSE

I stopped everything I was doing and took three long, deep breaths, in and out. I even yelled **"Pause"** for dramatic effect (because that's how I roll). I questioned my feelings at that moment and separated them from ME.

It's important to note that Feelings Aren't Facts, and they are Not Final, nor should we match our behavior to how we feel at that moment. Remember, we don't have to own everyone else's drama, unsafe beliefs, or demands, as they in no way define us or control us unless we give them permission to. Once we can grasp the fact that life is more of a *ME-WE* relationship built on a foundation of respect and boundaries, we can embrace life and its experiences with more purpose and intention and not take on more than we need to (or should for that matter) at any given moment.

Once I regained my power and acknowledged the Banana in the room (some might say elephant, but hey, this book is titled *It's Not About the Banana* for a reason), I was able to first and foremost *own* my part, which was: I should have fed the dog before I started work, set proper expectations of my timeline and boundaries with my family, and not responded to someone if I didn't have the time to reply.

Let me say that again: I should not have responded to someone if I didn't have the time to reply. Now, of course, this is more challenging in a face-to-face conversation, but practicing and enforcing boundaries is vital when you can. If the phone rings when you find yourself off your baseline, let it go to voicemail. If an email comes in and you don't have the mental capacity to respond with compassion and grace, don't respond. Give yourself time to regain your baseline first.

How do you know if you don't have the time to reply to someone, you ask?

If your response comes from a place of frustration, anger, or an inability to have compassion, then you know. Having boundaries and saying NO when we cannot give all of us is not selfish or rude; it is the complete opposite.

I've heard it said that we teach people how to treat us by how we treat ourselves, and this is a perfect example of that. If I don't value my time, why would someone else?

From here, I could realign my emotions, regain my sanity, and continue my day without resentments or judgments. I could give all of myself to the task or person at hand and feel present. I learned that day that life is always happening whether you are ready for it or not; however, I don't have to show up for all of it simultaneously.

Let's also not ignore or skip past the fact that, for some deep-rooted reason, I used to believe that I did.

Where did that come from?

PEEL

This is where we begin to recognize our own unsafe beliefs that we have been living as our truth, identify their original source, and once and for all remove the mind virus that has been keeping us sick. The overachieving, co-dependent, people-pleasing mentality that I had been living stemmed from a place of fear and lack. Fear that I wasn't good enough, that people didn't like me, and that if I was to be deemed worthy in life, I had to be successful and control the emotions of others to ensure they liked me.

REVEAL

Realizing that most of these false truths developed in my younger years of moving schools and being held back, struggling to make friends, and surrounding myself with people who didn't value their own worth, let alone mine, I could see how I could have adopted these erroneous beliefs.

HEAL

Being able to identify the root causes for my emotional response in the present moment, I could see how ridiculous and, better yet, just how outdated they were. To know that I was showing up in my present life as that same little six-year-old girl coloring outside the lines, I was able to see her, acknowledge her and love her for being who she was, and honor her by showing up for her today.

The best part about practicing the 5-Step Method is that you, too, can uncover your own erroneous and unsafe beliefs and start replacing them with safe ones. At any time or place in your life, you can Pause and Reset your Preset.

Your past has spoken, and it wants you to know it's time to let go. It's time to step into the YOU your future self has been preparing for. The time is now. Let's get to work!

Now let's find your baseline so we can get to the good stuff and Slay the Banana(s) in your life.

2

Finding Your Baseline

Step One: Baseline Preset

" You can't go back and change the beginning, but you can *"* start where you are and change the ending. ~C.S. **Lewis**

You'll want to get a journal for this exercise, as you will be recording details with the primary purpose of discovering your baseline and what moves it up or down. I also refer to this as our Preset.

I recommend finding a journal that speaks to you. Maybe it's your favorite color or has an inspirational quote that makes you smile. It doesn't need to cost a fortune to be special; I encourage you to find something just for this exercise and honor it, as it will be there to support you through this journey back to Self.

I started with a small composition book and have found a great hardcover one that I love and use to this day as I fine-tune and catch new patterns as I grow and expand my Emotional Diet. In fact, I'm working on turning it into an official "Emotional Fitness" Journal designed with this book in mind that will be available soon.

An Emotional Diet is everything we encounter in our day that we consume, digest, and process. What you watch, what you listen to, who you surround yourself with, and what you speak, think, and eat are all part of your emotional diet. As you evolve and become more awakened to your True Self, you will discover you need to change your diet. What used to satisfy you may start to cause you major heartburn and indigestion physically, mentally, and spiritually.

The more we become the person we are meant to be, the harder it is to continue living a life that no longer feeds and nourishes our souls.

Once you have your journal, follow these simple steps to find your baseline and uncover what pushes it off track.

First, you'll want to set THREE alarms on your phone and label them:

PAUSE

BREATHE

WHAT am I feeling?

If you notice, I didn't say *"HOW"* you are feeling. I find that when we say, "HOW are you feeling," our auto-response is set to say: "I'm feeling FINE."

FINE is not a feeling! Some say it's an acronym for F@ck'ed Up, Insecure, Neurotic, and Emotional.

Asking "WHAT" you feel permits us to describe the emotions.

Also, be intentional with the sound of the alarm you use for this exercise. I selected a calming alarm to initiate this therapeutic exercise and avoid jolting me into a panic before it even began. But hey, we all march to a different drum, so you do you and pick one that speaks to your *Soul.*

Helpful Tip:

Space the alarms out, selecting times that offer variation in your day.

Example:

I chose my first alarm to be my actual morning alarm, which I love as it reminds me right out of bed to be mindful, check in with my emotions, and *PAUSE* before I even start the day. Living my life with intention puts me on the right track and sets me up for a more fulfilling day.

Here, I can set my intentions for the day, then pay attention to my actions as I do my work. Without this first alarm, I can find my default setting kick in, which is to grab my phone, check Facebook and scroll through everyone else's dramas and traumas, see how many views I got on my last TikTok, pour a cup of coffee with ghee (yes, I put ghee in my coffee, don't judge), and get to work on those lovely emails. Instead, it is best to serve ME first, with my favorite morning routine of yoga, meditation, fresh juice, and journaling.

My next alarm is at noon, as I am usually knee-deep in life at this time, likely forgetting to BREATHE. For me, this alarm is set at the perfect time. I am reminded to be mindful of my thoughts and my body.

I take five slow, deep breaths in and out through my nose, as that is where and how we activate our parasympathetic nervous system, also known as our rest and digest system. If you're like me and find that your preset is not set to mindfulness, you live in your sympathetic nervous system 24/7, aka FIGHT OR FLIGHT.

This is the danger zone for our mind, body, and Soul. It's great when we are running from the lion chasing us for its dinner, but not so great when you are simply planning your own family's dinner.

My final reminder is at 4 p.m. when my workday is winding down and most of my family is home. I take a moment to check back in with myself by asking: "What am I feeling?"

I take some nice, long, relaxing deep breaths, in and out, and put pin holders in anything that needs my attention for later.

Remember, you can't be "everything" for "everyone" at all times.

Yes, that includes you too!

For the next two weeks, you will record your feelings and emotions, so keep this journal with you at all times.

Once the alarm goes off...

PAUSE

BREATHE

And ask yourself

What am I feeling?

Record your first thoughts and be real, raw, and honest. Let it all out and free write all the FEELS that are running your emotions at that moment.

One of my favorite teachers, *Gabby Bernstein*, calls it "Rage on the Page," which is so fitting for this exercise! Seriously, no one else will see this, so speak from your heart and let it all flow out and onto the paper.

Releasing it from you is also very therapeutic, as it removes the possible toxic energy from your body. Remember that feelings aren't FACTS; they are merely warning signs to pay attention to and service when needed.

But feelings are real, and I don't want to discount the fact that you have them. However, I do **not** want to give them more power than they should hold over you **ever**.

For most of us, our feelings are emotional armor hidden inside us from past trauma, drama, and stress. Or, as I like to say, other people's lies we chose to believe as our TRUTH. We hold onto it just in case we need to use it to fight that next battle, which always ends up being a battle within.

Like a food journal, you will record your Emotional Diet throughout the day. This is a judgment-free zone, and I can't stress that enough. Don't question, don't judge; just observe.

The goal is **not** to control your emotions at this point, nor is it to find fault in them. The goal is only to identify when they fluctuate.

Over the next two weeks you will have a wealth of information, signs, and triggers to identify in your life. These triggers you will later discover are your best teachers.

So enjoy this time of reconnecting to YOU. When I performed this exercise, I found that I felt as if I was coming out of a fog and gaining more clarity about who I am and what I needed to let go of to become "Her."

This exercise will help you do the same, one PEEL at a time.

Sorry, I couldn't resist a good banana pun.

3

The Power of the Pause

Step Two: Pause

> " Between stimulus and response, there is a space. In that "
> space is our power to choose our response. In our response
> lies our growth and freedom. ~Viktor Frankl

Now that you have established your baseline, let's look at the four emotional response types to identify your "preset" response. Just as important as it is to know what sets you off, it's equally important to understand how your body responds. Up until now, you have been interacting on autopilot. Understanding our response type helps us Reset our Preset to allow for a new experience and better outcome.

We've all heard about the Fight or Flight response. It is controlled by our Sympathetic Nervous System and activated within our Amygdala. This is where our emotional memories are stored. It ties our emotions to memories. This means that every time we encounter a situation in the present, we automatically identify it with an experience from our past. That past experience is what awakens the emotions linked to what you now feel in the present.

Without understanding and acknowledging our emotional response type, we are literally letting our past dictate our future. *Pausing* in the moment of stimulus, we are given an opportunity to choose differently.

Here is a list of the four most common emotional response types linked to Fight, Flight, Freeze, or Submit (a.k.a. Fawn).

Project (fight) is where we project undesirable feelings or emotions onto someone rather than admitting or dealing with the unwanted feelings. We project to avoid dealing with uncomfortable inner conflict and anxiety. We place the emotional discharge we experience onto someone else. *It's because of them that I am upset.*

Protect (submit/fawn) is abandoning your own needs to serve others to avoid conflict, rejection, or disapproval. You have trouble identifying your feelings to the point that you feel you have no identity or authentic self. You find yourself holding back your True Self for fear of abandonment, but, in the end, you end up abandoning yourself.

Deflect (freeze) is trying to feel less of whatever emotion we feel. We do everything other than feel and deal with the situation. We might find ourselves binging Netflix, scrolling TikTok for hours, overeating, over-drinking, or taking up our fifth new hobby.

Redirect (flight) is where we try to justify our actions and behaviors to reduce, avoid, or remove any negative consequences or outcomes. We try to diffuse an emotionally charged situation by watering down the actual event so it doesn't sound or feel as bad as it should. Or we avoid it altogether by changing our environment, ending a relationship, leaving a job, or relocating from the source to avoid or soften the situational outcome by justifying to ourselves that it was for the best.

Looking back to your journal, review the past three significant interactions with others that moved your baseline, or the most pressing problem you are facing today. What emotional response type from the list above do you identify with the most? Do you see a pattern in your emotional response? It is very common to see yourself in all four at different points in your life, but we usually identify ourselves with one *preset* response. For me, my preset response is Protect, with Deflect as a close second. It's my backup! Once we spot our go-to response, we can quickly link it to our emotions in the present and PAUSE.

The POWER of the PAUSE is a beautiful and magical tool.

Did you know that you have this POWER?

You do!

Before I knew I had it, I would find myself reacting, or, better yet, ***overreacting*** to everything and everyone that came my way. I would react, defend, and give my power away without question or thought. I lived a life fueled by emotional discharge, and most times, it backfired.

I would always find myself in a reactive state or defensive mode, not to mention that I had this need to achieve perfection in everything I did. I was always doing more than I should, signing up for more than I could handle, and saying yes to new things when I should have been saying no. It wasn't until I realized that I don't have to show up for everyone and respond to everything around me all at once that I could take back control of my life. (You may need to re-read that last sentence to let it sink in.)

The way I discovered this powerful gift within is an entirely different story, and one that I will share with you in hopes that you never have to experience what I went through.

STORYTIME

It was March 2020, and COVID had hit our state, Washington, and most of the world hard. Up until this point, we had all been watching the news and waiting to see if this was indeed going to be the moment we had been preparing for while watching *The Walking Dead* for the past 10 years. We were ready. I was prepared to stake out the local churches as a base camp and plan out who would be in our village of warriors to fend off the COVID zombie walkers.... I relaxed and released my claim on the local church, however, once we knew we would not bleed out of our eyeballs.

I began working from home as we faced our first lockdown, stocked up on supplies, and only took my fair share of toilet paper. (Seriously, what was up with the toilet paper?) Just like that, I gave up on my morning routine of yoga, meditation, juicing, and journaling, and traded it in for early morning Zoom meetings, counting the COVID infection ticker on my computer toolbar, and listening to talk radio playing in the background. I was obsessed with staying informed and consumed with what the lockdown meant for my family, school, work, and lifestyle. My 21-year-old son was now staying with me and my husband, as well as our youngest daughter. And none of them could go anywhere.

Let me tell you; I started to flat line. LITERALLY.

I was stressing about everything and everyone, trying to control every situation that could happen, might happen, or may never happen, but OMG, what if it *did* happen? It was I-need-to-plan-for-it-type stressing. My son was one that, for whatever reason, I hyper-focused on. *(Deflect Response.)* He needed a plan, a future, and a new way of thinking, and

I was determined and convinced that it was the Navy. For two weeks straight, I had Tony Robbins-type talks with him, trying to ignite the flame within him to take massive action and join the Navy. Yet day after day, *NOTHING*...No spark, no flame, no flicker. Nothing.

My other children were 13 and 18, both girls. The 13-year-old had just left elementary school and was barely in junior high before school was canceled indefinitely for her. The 18-year-old was lucky enough to have graduated before COVID could take that away from her, but she missed her college graduation as she worked hard to finish college early to start her career as a hairdresser. She was devastated. My oldest son was barely breathing, (figuratively) my husband never missed a beat of work, and my youngest daughter was now being introduced to TikTok, which would later become her junior high experience and an example of how teenagers behave. It was a S*!T SHOW, for which I tried my best to organize the lights; dress the characters; write, produce, and act out all the scenes... until that magical day when the lights went out.

It was April 4, 2020, and we had just returned from a nice walk around the neighborhood and had started to make dinner. I had been feeling off for months now, but today was different. I felt light-headed and dizzy, and had this strange pressure inside my neck. I could feel my blood pressure racing thru my veins, and I knew something wasn't right. After dinner, I remember sitting next to my husband in the living room, where we had all retired to watch a movie. As I opened my sparkling water, I recall getting ready to take the first sip. I said to my husband, "Babe, I feel weird." I went to take that sip, spilled it on myself, and said, "Oh, just lovely Tonya."

And that was that.

The next thing I knew I was in an ambulance with two men looking down at me, saying, "Everything is fine; you just had a seizure, and your husband is following behind us." What the HOLY HELL was going on? I had a SEIZURE? How was this even possible? I had never been healthier. I quit drinking (two years sober at this point) and quit smoking (one year smoke-free at this point), and I was working out every day, eating healthy, and meditating daily! How could I have had a SEIZURE?

It took about a month before my brain came back online completely and another three months of testing to discover that I was healthy and nothing was wrong with me. Excuse me? I had a SEIZURE. How could nothing be wrong with me when I had a SEEEIIIIZUUUURRRE? But that is what the doctors continued to say, test after test after test. My heart looked good; my brain was good, minus the few lesions that I'm sure had something to do with drinking half my body weight in wine a day (okay, all my body weight, but I'll save that for another chapter). I was given a clean bill of health.

My blood work was the only thing my doctor could point to that showed I wasn't perfect—my potassium levels were low, so he prescribed a potassium supplement and called it a day. Now I mean no disrespect to my doctor or any doctors out there, but WTF? I had a SEIZURE, and the only thing that was possibly off was my potassium levels, which *may* cause you to feel dizzy? But causing a SEIZURE? The question *now* was WHY were my potassium levels off?

Of course, being the health nut I am, I had to dig deeper, so I consulted with my Ayurveda professor and got to the root of the problem, which is the goal of this book—to help you get to the root. When we mask our symptoms with substances and external noise like *booze, food, sex, shopping, gambling, etc.*, we might feel better at the moment, or appear as if everything is okay on the outside. But the instant the masks are removed, we are left vulnerable, weak, and exposed to the Truth.

For most of us, facing the Truth is too ugly, too hard, or too much work to deal with. Instead, we avoid; we run and cover it up with pills, partners, wine, and other band-aids, hoping it will heal or go away without any work or attention. We survive rather than thrive. We allow our survival instincts to run the show. Unfortunately, that is not how real healing works. You must get to the root, pull it out, and treat it before you can truly heal. So that's what I did; I discovered I had a "leaky gut," so I healed my gut lining so it could heal me! It worked. (Again, I'm sure it was from all the classy high-grade box wine I was consuming.) I didn't need to take anti-seizure medication or potassium supplements to maintain homeostasis or avoid having another SEIZURE. I had to get to the root and water it.

In reality, I don't think low potassium was the causing factor that created the perfect storm for my body to glitch and short circuit. The toxic environment I was allowing myself to be in was just as bad, if not worse. I gave up my morning routine and traded it in for drama and stress. *(Redirect Response.)* I started to act "as if" I had all the control and refused to surrender. I became a victim of the toxic environment in which I chose to place myself.

I once heard someone say that you cannot play the victim when you are a *willing* participant. *I felt that hard!*

I've now come to appreciate the power of the PAUSE more than ever. I have found true inner peace in knowing that the Universe does have my back. I don't have to do all the things to prove my worth, nor do I have to solve all life's problems to have a purpose. In this PAUSE, we regain control of our emotions and actions. We can see that there are no obstacles in life; only opportunities to grow, learn, and gain awareness. Even COVID became a bittersweet blessing for me.

You'll hear me say many times that the Universe does for us, what we will not do for ourselves, and sometimes that means forcing us to pause in order to reset. This is where we find blessings in the pain and regain a new perspective toward the obstacles presented and turn them into opportunities for growth.

We have an opportunity in this PAUSE to acquire new tools and experiences to help us uncover our true purpose and fine-tune our talents.

Yes, talents!

We all have a unique set of gifts and talents. Most of us haven't discovered them yet because we've been living in survival mode. When we discredit the power of the PAUSE, we become vulnerable and fall prey to low vibrational energy (stress, negativity, drama, gossip, greed, jealousy, sloth) and miss this opportunity to grow. Instead, we find ourselves stuck in a negative habit loop and continue repeating it... repeatedly.

We've all heard it said a million times, and for the sake of dramatic PAUSE...

"The definition of insanity is doing the same thing over and over again, expecting a different result."

It's time to shift to something that better serves us. It's time to start calling your own shots, recruiting the right players to your team (Shift Shapers), and, once and for all, start living YOUR TRUTH! Life is always happening around you whether you participate in it or not, so how you choose to show up matters. Even more important is how you choose to play with the shots and opportunities you've been given. Going back to the story of my life being a S*!T SHOW when I allowed life to play me, I was choosing to show up as a victim of my circumstances and not see the opportunities it was providing me if I had only PAUSED.

How do you do this, you ask?

PAUSE when agitated!

When you feel off your baseline...

PAUSE.

Take three long, deep breaths, in and out.

Identify your emotional response, and this might go without saying, but I'm going to say it anyways...

Exhale!

The next chapter will go over just what we do in this PAUSE that will change the course of our life and how we show up for it today.

Meditation for Anxiety

I release the stress of yesterday.

I release, I release

I let go of the worries of tomorrow.

I let go, I let go

Today I will live in the present.

I embrace my power within

I embrace, I embrace.

Today I face my problems and live in the solution.

Here is where I find my strength

Here is where I find my courage

Today I surrender

Today I am at peace

Essential Oils for Emotional Well-Being

Lavender:

- Anti-depressive.
- Balancing and Purifying for Mind, Body, and Emotions.
- Reduces Irritability.
- Reduces Emotional Overload.
- Relieves Worry

Orange:

- Removes Stress.
- Calms Nervousness.
- Releases Anxiety.

Neroli:

- Alleviates Sadness.
- Calms Anxiety Attacks.
- Clears Mental and Emotional Blocks.
- Clears the Path to Looking Within.

4

Peel to Feel

Step Three: Peel

It's in allowing ourselves to become uncomfortable that we become comfortable.

Once you have found yourself off your baseline and have hit *PAUSE*, the next step is to *PEEL*. First, envision peeling or detaching yourself away from the situation that has currently moved your baseline. If possible, physically remove yourself from the room, end the call, or STOP typing/texting. This is not an emotional response; it's more of a safety response. It's best to do nothing when unsure what and why your baseline has moved. Taking another set of three deep, cleansing breaths to bring us back to our bodies, we are ready to PEEL another layer.

It's time to PEEL TO FEEL.

Oh yes, you read that correctly; I said feel. Now, before you throw down the book and look for your receipt to return it, keep reading. I promise this won't hurt; well, maybe a little, but I swear it will be worth it. My husband jokes around a lot about stuffing his feelings deep down inside where no one can find them, and most of the time, I laugh. However, it's not all that funny when you think about it.

Most people do just that. They stuff, avoid, and run away from their feelings, hoping they will disappear or resolve on their own. That stuffing keeps us stuck, makes us sick, and disconnects us from our Soul-Self. Instead of feeling it, we create more layers of armor that block us from the light of our truth. No wonder addiction, depression, mental illness, and suicide are facing an all-time HIGH in our world.

Instead of avoiding the things that are moving our baseline and attacking it with anger, or covering it up with other things such as drinking, shopping, sex, or whatever your guilty pleasure of choice is, we are going to PAUSE and PEEL back the armor to get to the root of the problem.

I'd also like to mention that you are NOT your triggers, and it is time we face those people, places, and things that lower your vibration and leave you feeling like a victim, helpless, doomed to fail, or unworthy of love. It's time you take your beautiful SUPER POWER back and use it to heal you and others like you. Put that on a sticky note all over your house, in your car, at your desk, or wherever it will catch your attention daily. I can't say it enough, YOU ARE WORTH THE SPACE, and you are made to love and be loved.

I don't doubt that peeling back the banana might expose some vulnerability you've been hiding from or trying to ignore. Because you must *feel it to heal it*, you may want some loving reminders of how amazing you are. Placing positive love notes to yourself all around your house, on your phone, in your car, and wherever you spend time is important, as we are our own worst critics and enemies. We can be harder on ourselves than we realize.

When you've been playing the support role your entire life, it takes time to adjust to the lead role you were born to play. Peeling back the armor causing you to feel off your baseline takes practice and time, so give yourself plenty of grace during this process. Remember, this is your life to live, and you get to call the shots and decide how you will show up at this moment and every moment to follow.

With permission from my friends, family, and clients, I will share their stories within the Five-Step Method to provide examples of how this process works in real-life situations, starting with my friend Scott. He was having a rough go at life and feeling like nothing was ever going his way; as if the Universe was out to get him. Because of his way of thinking, he struggled to find a relationship and nearly quit his job.

One day at work, he showed up to find someone else working at his station. He was immediately thrown off his baseline and fell into that negative thinking loop of life isn't fair; nobody likes him, no one respects his space, and his boss must want to fire him. He went into the break room, where he overheard a second-hand story of him being slow in the process line he was working in.

"See, I was right! My boss wants me fired!" he said to himself.

Gossip had validated his feelings; he overheard other people talking about what they had overheard.

Sounds solid!

He quickly messaged me, saying that he hates his job and the people he works for and that they all want him gone.

Now to you and I, we can see the overreaction a mile away, but in that moment, he was so off his baseline that he couldn't see the Truth if it hit him in the face.

"Scott," I said, "It's not about the Banana." Once we understand the energy behind that phrase and its healing properties, just saying it can make you feel better.

As soon as he realized he was most certainly off his baseline and got caught up in the negative thinking loop of unsafe beliefs, he was able to PAUSE, take a few deep, cleansing breaths through his nose to activate his parasympathetic nervous system, and slowly PEEL back the emotions he was experiencing. Once we calm our minds and remove ourselves from the emotional attachment we created, we can ask ourselves a few simple questions:

What am I feeling?

Why am I feeling this way?

Is this true?

If it is true, can I change it?

If I can change it, what do I need to do right now to change it?

Then Act!

Remember, feelings aren't facts; they are feelings. Feelings are emotions linked to a past experience. As much as we need to honor and acknowledge our feelings, we must also accept that our feelings may be outdated or simply not true. They could be outdated because the last time you experienced this emotion could have been when you were a little kid and didn't get picked for dodgeball, or when you got dumped or turned down for a job. Chances are that emotional memory response has not caught up to the present you.

In Scott's situation, he first felt anger when he saw a new co-worker setting up in his station. He immediately assumed it was because his boss wanted him fired. Once he could acknowledge that his anger came from a place of false evidence appearing real, he could let go of this emotion and accept a different possible explanation. This guy was new and maybe didn't realize that he was at the wrong station, or perhaps his boss had assigned him to another station that day to change things up in the production line. Peeling back even deeper, Scott had felt like he wasn't good enough at his job, so he was constantly entering the warehouse feeling less than his coworkers. Again, I can't stress this enough— feelings aren't FACTS...just because Scott is feeling less than, we know for a FACT that this is not true. Once Scott was able to go through the questions, he was able to *reset* his *preset*.

What am I feeling? *Hot, tense, heart racing.*

Why am I feeling this way? The n*ew guy is taking my job.*

Is this true? *I don't know.*

If it is true, can I change it? *No.*

If it isn't true, can I acknowledge the feeling and let it go? *Yes.*

If I can change it, what is it that I can do at this moment? *Ask the new guy if he needs help setting up his new station.*

Then Act!

Scott did just that. And, in fact, the gentleman was indeed in the wrong station. Scott helped welcome him and set him up in his correct area. Even better, Scott found out that the guy talking bad about him and spreading rumors was written up for being slow on the line and was trying to blame other people for not hitting his numbers. (**Projection Response.**)

It had NOTHING to do with Scott, and he was about to walk away from a job that, in fact, was his dream job. Today, Scott is still working at the same place and continues to practice Steps 3 and 4 daily. For many of us, these can be the harder of the steps, as they deal with acknowledgment, acceptance, and letting go of unsafe beliefs that no longer serve us.

The PEEL and REVEAL steps take practice. When your *preset* is set to survival mode, it takes time to *reset*. That is why the PAUSE step is so important. The pause allows you to breathe and center yourself, bringing you back to the present. It allows you the time needed to assess what is really moving your baseline. The PAUSE gives you a chance to acknowledge the emotion. Peeling back will enable you to identify your emotion and put it in its proper place, which empowers you to respond in a healthy and healing way.

When we remove the distraction that initiated the imbalance, we can dive deeper into the truth—redirecting our attention to the root cause of our emotional discharge. Accepting that the emotional response has nothing to do with the present but the past, we acknowledge the source.

True healing is dealing with our feelings instead of feeding them.

Meditation for Insight

Universe, grant me the willingness to see where I am, not

To say I can't is to say I am unwilling

Today I am willing

Today I am willing to embrace the uncomfortable and give myself
permission to grow

Today I am willing

Today I am willing to try new things

Today I am willing to think new thoughts

Today I am willing to feel the fear and lean toward faith

Today I am willing to experience new emotions

Today I am willing to challenge my unsafe beliefs

Today I am willing

Today I am

Essential Oils for Clarity and Strength

Orange:

- Sweeps Away Negativity.
- Repairs Damage to the Auric Field.
- Enlivening
- Uplifting

Helichrysum:

- Spiritual Integration in the Physical World.
- Adapt to Change to Find Purpose and Inner Peace.
- Promotes Strength to Undertake a Journey of Self-Discovery.

Jasmine:

- Increases Self-Confidence.
- Optimism
- Well-being.
- Heightens Spiritual Awareness.
- Inspires Hope, Joy, Openness, and Love.

5

Reveal to Heal

Step Four: Reveal

> " Maybe the journey isn't so much about becoming any- "
> thing, maybe it's about un-becoming everything that isn't
> really you so you can be who you were meant to be.
>
> ~Paulo Coelho

As I mentioned at the end of Chapter Four, The REVEAL and HEAL steps can be some of the more challenging steps, as they deal with acknowledgment, acceptance, and letting go of people, places, things, and unsafe beliefs that no longer serve you. Holding onto old beliefs or false narratives is what keeps you stuck, sick, and destined to repeat the same mistakes over and over again.

Emotions are the ultimate resource for growth. The patterns of your emotions dictate your life. What we experience and the emotions linked to that experience directly reflect our life as it is today. Your Emotional Fitness is more important than your emotional intelligence. Have a beginner's mindset. Hit the reset button and start questioning everything with a beginner's mind. Everything. Be open-minded to learn and unlearn, to understand and expand your awareness. Did I mention unlearn?

The first way we do this is by separating you from the experience. Bad things happened to you. You may have even done bad things. But **you are not a bad person.** You messed up. **You are not a mess up.** You failed. **You are not a failure.** You made a mistake. **YOU ARE NOT A MISTAKE.** You may have an illness, but **you are not the illness**; you may have a health diagnosis, but **you are not the diagnosis.** Whatever the label, diagnosis, past mistake, or otherwise, **YOU ARE NOT IT!**

But how do you know what to let go of and what to keep? What is serving you, and what is holding you back? What is keeping you stuck or sick, and what is feeding your Soul? Chances are if it makes you want to Deflect, Protect, Project, or Redirect, it's probably something to address. Your best gauge on this is your gut. If it feels heavy or makes you feel less than, it's probably hurting you more than serving your highest good. They don't say "Trust Your Gut" for nothing!

Another way to tell where our unsafe beliefs lie is in our vocabulary. Pay attention to the thoughts you think and the words you speak. Your "gut" is always talking and will be sure to let you know what is contaminated, expired, or sour. When we feel sick to our stomach at a thought, memory, or current event, chances are we are thinking of an unsafe belief at that very moment. Also, they usually involve the words should, could, would, always, and never.

Some most common unsafe beliefs are:

1. I'm not good enough.
2. I should've known better.
3. I will never make it.
4. People always let me down or leave.
5. I can never depend on others.

Understanding that even though feelings aren't FACTS, they are linked to a past event that was very REAL to you at the time. But *then* is not *now*. Now is now, and it's time to experience life in the now, not yesterday's now.

Here's how...

Now hear me out—I'm about to get a little scientific on you for a second. (Well, as scientific as I can get, anyways.) I want to talk more about the Amygdala, which is a section of our brain that helps define and regulate emotions. It also preserves memories and attaches them to specific emotions without our permission. It activates the fight or flight response, which is also done without our consent. This response is triggered by emotions such as stress, fear, anxiety, and anger that have been linked to PRIOR experiences.

Do you see where I am going with this? We then have the frontal lobes responsible for reasoning, thinking, and decision-making. They allow you to evaluate your emotions and use your experiences and judgment to respond consciously. Notice the word "consciously." Yes, this is the part where you have control. However, when your Amygdala gets hijacked, that voluntary response gets shut off. This hijacking occurs when we continue to allow our emotions to run the show. This is why Emotional Fitness is more important than Emotional Intelligence.

When we don't PAUSE before taking action, we react. It's in the "reacting" that our Amygdala's response is supported and validated to the point that it doesn't even allow your frontal lobes to have an opinion. The more our Amygdala is validated in our reactions, the farther away we are from our Truth. Reacting is the perfect description of this behavior. We are playing out a previous emotional memory in the present. Hence "Re-Acting." These false beliefs we have adopted from past experiences are creating our reality in the present.

A fun game I started to play with myself whenever I was asked if I wanted to do something, eat something, wear something, show up for something, be a part of something, or whatever it may have been that I was asked to do, if I was quick to say NO, turn up my nose, or quickly disengage, I made myself PAUSE and then asked myself:

Why am I so quick to say no or disconnect?

What am I afraid will happen if I say yes?

What is it about the situation that is off-putting?

What am I resisting?

Why?

I started to challenge my PRESET of saying NO and started to say YES. It could have been something as small and silly as saying no to tomatoes on my salad, I don't like sushi, or I will never swim in the ocean. I never gave it much thought until, one day, I did.

STORYTIME

After years of avoiding sushi nights with my family, I am now the one saying, "Let's get sushi for dinner." The fact was that I had only tried sushi once, 10 years ago, and hated the taste of seaweed, and swore sushi off forever. Once I allowed myself to try it again, I found that I loved sushi. I still don't like the taste of seaweed, but little did I know sushi comes in all different forms and flavors.

With the first little win under my belt, I decided it was time to swim with the big dogs, aka my family, in the ocean of Hawaii. Having been blessed to travel there on a few occasions, you would find my husband diving for treasure and the kids wave-jumping while I lay perfectly safe under my oversized umbrella, observing. Deep down, I wished I could join in the fun and experience what they were enjoying, but I was too scared. My fear of sharks grew stronger every year, to the point that I could barely dip my toe in the water. However, this time I was saying YES to new experiences.

After a few days of staring out at my family having fun wave-jumping, and at my husband snorkeling for sea turtles, I mustered up the courage to dip my toe in the water of fear. While my family watched in amazement, I slowly wadded my way to "death by shark." I took a step, then another, then another. Before I knew it, I was swimming. Well, more like letting the waves take me out and bring me back to shore, but I was swimming. The fear of being eaten by a shark slowly left my body, and I was, for the first time in more than a decade, experiencing Hawaii with my family through their eyes while creating new memories in the process... until something brushed up against my leg!

OMG, it was a shark! I quietly removed myself from the ocean to find my husband staring at me with a puzzled look on his face. He asked me what I was doing, and I whispered, "I think a shark touched me." He looked down into the murky water of horror to find a beautiful sea turtle passing by. Yes, a sea turtle rubbed up against me, not a shark. Once I regained my composure, I slowly and cautiously wadded back into the water, just enough to catch a glimpse of the majestic wonder. It was indeed a sea turtle, and it was swimming toward me. It came up to me and poked its head out of the water, and, I kid you not, our eyes made contact, and I swear he said to me, "Everything is going to be okay."

The calm and serenity I experienced is something I will never forget. At that moment, I realized that fear is the pathway to faith. When we feel the fear but walk toward it anyway, we will be met with gifts beyond our wildest dreams. We will find strength where we once felt weak, blessings where there once was pain, and answers to the lessons we finally showed up to learn.

One thing my husband still wanted to know was that if it *was* a shark, why did I *quietly* remove myself, and not save my family? Truth be told, I know I can be a bit of a drama queen, so I felt it was best to swim in my shame alone. Deep down, I knew it wasn't a shark, but the fear was too real for my body to accept. My mind said stay, but my body said nope. My fear response was so deeply wired that the minute I felt uncomfortable, I ran, even though I knew it wasn't a shark.

That sea turtle taught me so much that day, lessons I would have never learned if I didn't dare to take that first step.

1. I don't have to swim in my shame alone.
2. It's okay to be scared; just don't let it paralyze you from living.
3. Our emotional response is linked to a past trauma we need to heal.
4. You can run on water.

I later came to find that sea turtles symbolize protection, emotional strength, and healing, all of which were revealed to me that day.

> *Most times, we say NO to avoid being uncomfortable. Don't confuse comfort for safety.*

Coming home from that spiritual experience in Hawaii changed my life for the better in more ways than I have space to mention in this book. After testing the waters on my new theory, I wanted to dive even deeper. In fact, later that same year, I had many more revelations that I want to share with you.

The first experience I want to share is a difficult one. It was honestly the hardest pill for me to swallow, as it was so deeply rooted within my core that exposing its ugly Truth and facing it head-on was extremely hard for me to do.

It had to do with money.

Growing up poor as a child, I always longed for *more*. Be it a nice house, a car I wasn't ashamed to be seen in, or clothes I wasn't embarrassed to wear, I was determined to make my own money to be able to afford the things I longed for as a child. Yet as soon as I started to obtain these things, I would quickly sabotage my situation and lose it all. I did this multiple times to the point that I assumed I was meant to be poor and struggle. I adopted this as my truth and it became the bar I set for myself. As Tony Robbins says, we always rise to the bar we set for ourselves, and, apparently, I set the bar at bankruptcy, debt, and a less-than-flattering credit score.

After years of struggling to save a penny, or to rebuild that credit score (again) after another wild decade of financial debauchery, I was finally making decent money. Like, *really good* money. And, even better... year-end bonuses. I was paying off bills, raising my credit score every month, and actually saving money (if you call the dollar round-up free service the banks offer nowadays saving money, then, technically, I was saving money... progress, not perfection, people). I had it all figured out and was simultaneously living the good life and loving life.

It wasn't until I challenged myself to this new game of "If I usually say NO, I must say YES" that I realized I was experiencing Identity Sabotage all over again. I didn't think I was doing this, as I was paying my bills and saving money. Sure, I wasn't saving as I should have, but I was saving nonetheless, and I wasn't doing anything bad other than spending more than I should on random Amazon things. But who doesn't do that? I mean, the dog needed that cute food dish/water bowl combo stand to keep her food bowls off the floor, and I needed those super cute hanging crochet plant basket holders for my new office, and... well, you get the picture. I was spending more than I needed to, but man was I feeling good.

Until I wasn't.

I was sitting there, writing out a limiting belief I had about myself. It was centered around starting my own business, "The Soul Shack," but I couldn't realize this dream just yet because I—you guessed it—didn't have enough money. Then I remembered that every time a financial money savings lecture came on for school, I would start multi-tasking and avoid *really* paying attention. I would tell myself that I don't need to hear it, or it doesn't apply to me, because I *have* money...what a load of crap.

The Truth was that I feared money. I was scared that I would never have enough of it, or I would lose what I did have, so I never respected it.

Why bother? I was living in an old belief system that no longer served me. I'm not sure if that one ever served me, but it was more apt to serve me when I was living paycheck to paycheck. Savings? What savings? Credit? What's that? Now that I could see my disconnect and lack of respect toward money, I could pay attention to my emotional currency. I signed up for money classes and even bought a book titled *Emotional Currency: A Woman's Guide to Building a Healthy Relationship with Money* by Kate Levinson, Ph.D. I highly recommend it.

Another example of me saying YES when my mind was quick to say NO was when I attended a four-day workshop, and every day they brought out fun, fit, and fabulous dancers full of energy, excitement, and plenty of cool moves. I instantly left the room or avoided it at all costs. I went to the bathroom, refilled my water, reviewed my notes from the night before; I even sat there and stared at them with disgust and judgment. Seriously, I hate to admit it, but I did. I was that girl. Until I wasn't.

I had to take a long, hard look in the mirror and ask myself why I was so against this type of exercise. What about it was putting me off? Then it hit me—I wanted to be them and feel free to move my body and dance like no one was watching, just like I did when I was drinking and dancing at the bar.

Even deeper, I discovered that I only danced when I was drinking, for fear of being judged is no longer a concern when you're hammered. I went back another layer to when I was cut (for the second time) when trying out for the Seagals, the cheer squad for the Seattle Seahawks. I was rejected by a group of ladies that I used to feel so much a part of in high school when I was a cheerleader. I wrote it off as not being good enough and resolved to let that dream go. I let it go all right.... up to this moment where I was staring, glaring, and judging these beautiful souls loving their healthy bodies and wanting to share that with others to do the same. I hadn't danced in more than 10 years. WTF? Once I could see why I ran from the thought of dancing or expressing myself through dance, I could ask myself the questions.

What am I feeling? *Anxious, tense, and uncomfortable!*

Why do you feel this way? *Because they are doing something I wish I could do. I'm jealous.*

Is it true? *No.*

If it's not true, what can you do to change it? *Register for the classes and participate.*

Once I determined what I could do at that moment to change, I took action. I signed up for dance lessons and have been loving it ever since. I'll say it again, in case you missed it at the beginning of the previous chapter:

> It's in allowing ourselves to become uncomfortable that we become comfortable.

The examples of my old story no longer serving me today are just a sample of what you can experience when you start facing the Bananas in your life by applying these simple yet effective steps and strategies. When you surrender to whatever it is that you are resisting, fighting, or trying to ignore and face its Truth and deal with it— it no longer has power over you. Nowadays, when I see the Truth and the Lie exposed, I always say I have two choices:

Eat the Banana or Die!

Yes, being a drama queen is still one of my unsafe beliefs that I see as an asset, so I'm keeping it for now. Progress is still progress. Plus, when we look at it from a metaphor standpoint, if we are not growing, we are slowly dying.

Step Four, REVEAL, will expose some ugly Truths and unsafe beliefs we have come to believe about ourselves and others. Rest easy in knowing you do not have to continue believing them today. First, PAUSE when agitated, discontent, or disturbed and take three long, cleansing breaths. Second, ask yourself the important emotions check questions, starting with "What am I feeling?" And third, see the Truth and the Lie exposed and either **eat the Banana** or... go back to Step One!

For those of you who thought I would say **die**, I love you! But in all seriousness, when we are ready to Eat the Banana, we begin to Heal, which brings us to Step Five.

Meditation for Forgiveness

Left hand on heart, Right hand on stomach

Today I accept me, All of me

Today I accept my Truth

I breathe in Truth

I exhale Doubt

I breathe in Truth

I exhale Fear

I breathe in Truth

I exhale Worry

I breathe in Compassion

I exhale Judgment

I breathe in Joy

I exhale Anger

I breathe in Hope

I exhale Despair

Essential Oils for Forgiveness and Compassion

Neroli:

- Eases Mental and Emotional Tension.
- Helps with Depression
- Emotional Balancing.

Myrrh:

- Helps Dissipate the Feelings of Sadness to Release Emotions to go Forward in Life.
- Boosts Confidence.
- Lifts Mood.
- Promotes Peace and Tranquility.
- Settles an Overactive Mind.

Bergamot:

- Reduces Anger.
- Addresses Insecurity.
- Reduces Fear.
- Helps with PTSD.
- Encourages the Release of Pent-up Feelings.

6

Heal to Thrive

Step Five: Heal

> The roadmap to *Enlightenment* is through learning techniques that help you heal along the way.

One of the most powerful ways to promote inner healing is to Surrender. Many of us spend our entire life fighting and resisting it. We beat ourselves up trying to control the things we cannot change and end up convincing ourselves it is because we are not good enough, smart enough, pretty enough, or worthy enough to change them. We use all the excuses, reasons, and justifications as to why we are where we are, hoping it will provide some ease and comfort. It never does. Why? Because most of us are living a lie.

The biggest lie we tell ourselves when we don't reach a goal or obtain something we want in life is to say that we "self-sabotage." This type of thinking brings us back to believing we are unworthy of whatever it is we desire, so we sabotage ourselves from ever fully obtaining it. "Self-sabotage" implies we know ourselves. But if we truly knew ourselves, we would see that we are incapable of sabotage. We have become so disconnected from our Truth that we don't realize how powerful, deserving, and worthy we are. "Identity Sabotage" is more appropriate. The true identity of our spiritual being has been sabotaged.

To heal from Identity Sabotage, we must first Surrender to what we think we know. Learn and unlearn who it is we think we are. The stories we tell ourselves and the ideals we place on ourselves need to be abandoned. We must let go of who we "think" we need to be and Surrender to the spiritual being we were born to become.

Life is not a competition; it's a collaboration. We spent most of our lives trying to fit in when we were made to stand out. Once we can surrender to this fact and stop fighting life, we can finally start living *our* life.

Knowing what you know now, how can you change how you see the current Bananas in your life? How can you change your perspective and ask yourself, "What is this trying to teach me?" Or "How is this trying to change me?" Or "What am I resisting that I am actually missing?" I've found that what we resist persists for a good reason.

Remember that life is giving you everything that you need to succeed. When we miss the message or resist its lessons, it might go away for a day, a week, a month, or even a year. Heck, sometimes more if you are stubborn like I was. But one thing is certain—no matter how hard you try to avoid it, life, a.k.a. the Universe, will bring it back until you finally accept it and surrender to its lessons. Most of these lessons are blessings given to us through other people. I call them Shift Shapers. Not to be confused with Shape Shifters; that is not what I am talking about when I say SHIFT Shaper.

A Shift Shaper is someone who literally helps you SHIFT. You are either the Shift Shaper or are in the presence of one at any given moment. The Universe is always sending the right people and experiences into your life to help you evolve into the person you are meant to be. This includes how you show up in other people's lives as well.

Sometimes you are their lesson, other times, they are yours, but most times, you are both simultaneously. These people have something to share, give, and teach us that will help us *shift* into a higher frequency and connect to our authentic self, our Soul-Self, and our purpose. When I think back to all the Shift Shapers in my life, it gives me goosebumps.

Resistance is an excellent indicator of an unresolved or misplaced emotion and a glimpse into your true identity. I connected with a few immediately; others I didn't realize were Shift Shapers until years later, and some I resisted altogether. What we resist persists, so be mindful of what you are avoiding.

One of my favorite Shift Shapers, besides the turtle, is Gabby Bernstein. I was heavy into my spiritual awakening journey, and she kept popping up everywhere I turned. At first, I didn't pay much attention, but after a while, it became apparent that the Universe was trying to send me a message. It wouldn't be long before the one I resisted the most appeared again, and once I acknowledged her and connected to her energy, I shifted.

STORYTIME

I was at Barnes & Noble, searching for a book that *called to me*. This was something I would frequently do; I love walking down the isles looking at all the authors, titles, and fun covers, allowing myself to be drawn in to a book. Most times, my soul would pull me to the self-help area, but on occasion, I would find myself lost in the travel section.

I looked at all the travel books of places I longed to go and found myself drawn to a book on Bali. I picked up the book, and behind it was another book with Gabby's face on it. For those of you who don't know who Gabby is, she doesn't write travel books. Yet there she was, looking at me AGAIN! I took the book and walked it over to where it belonged, because that is what a responsible book nerd would do. While I walked, I conducted a full-on conversation with her (thankfully, it was in my head).

I looked her right in the eyes and asked her WHY she kept showing up in my life? What did she have to teach me that I haven't already learned from Wayne Dyer, Louise Hay, and other spiritual teachers I admire?

What I heard back was one of the most profound intuitive hits I have ever received.

"I am the part of you that you don't want to see but must."

Message received, and I would be lying if I said it didn't hurt. The Truth was that I had been avoiding her books and resisting her message because I was jealous. She triggered all my fears, doubts, and limiting beliefs within me. I was filled with judgment about myself and displaced it onto her.

The emotional response I was exhibiting was **Projection.**

We project to protect. We project to avoid dealing with uncomfortable inner conflict and anxiety. My unsafe belief system justified my avoidance of her. Once I allowed myself to see the Truth behind my resistance, I shifted. The Universe sent me a message that, as Gabby would say, punctured me where I needed healing the most. I saw in her what I didn't see in myself—confidence, self-worth, charisma, and purpose. She had what I wanted but didn't feel worthy of receiving.

The Truth and the Lie were exposed.

Truth: *I am worthy. Denying it doesn't make it less true. It is only my Ego that blocks me.*

versus

Lie: *I am not good enough.*

I had two choices:

Eat the Banana or Die.

I chose to eat the Banana and bought that book.

Over the next couple of years I had the opportunity to speak with Gabby on multiple occasions; was on her podcast; and was gifted one of her courses, "Spirit Junkie Master Class," that she felt called to give me after a powerful breakthrough she helped me overcome. Even more, she inspired me to write and fully embrace that I am a writer, capable of doing what I feel called to do.

What was the name of that book I found misplaced in Barnes & Noble that day, you ask?

The Universe Has Your Back

I know, right? Like, seriously, you can't make this stuff up!

So don't worry if you have repeatedly been avoiding a particular Shift Shaper in your life; the Universe, a.k.a. life, will keep presenting them to you until you are finally ready to let them in.

Every time I am quick to say no to something or resist someone, I ask myself why?

What is it about that person, place, or thing to which I am saying no?

What am I trying to avoid, hide, or deny?

The answers have surprised me, and I have no doubt they will surprise you, too.

I've discovered some false truths about myself and have faced some fears I didn't realize I had. For me, I have found that fear is the pathway to faith. Sometimes we say no to avoid being uncomfortable, but it's in the act of being uncomfortable that we can finally become comfortable.

Question everything and practice having a beginner's mind in everything you do or don't do. Dare to grow. Dare to try new things, or even revisit the old ones. What served you yesterday may not serve you today, so be mindful of what you resist. Surrendering is the quickest way to heal. We find our true strength, power, and purpose by accepting and surrendering to our weaknesses.

How do you do it, you ask?

Simply apply the Five-Step Method every time you find yourself triggered. I wish I could find a word that is less triggering than trigger, but then it wouldn't be as triggering.

That being said, it is essential to know a few things:

1. You are not your triggers.
2. Triggers are your teachers.
3. Labels do not define you.
4. You are not a byproduct.

Words are powerful, and we must pay attention to the words we choose to give our power. Words are linked to feelings, memories, and, as we now know, our emotional discharge. When misused, they form unsafe beliefs and steal our identity. Whoever said sticks and stones might break my bones, but words will never hurt me, never understood the power of the Word. Just read the book *The Four Agreements* by Don Miguel Ruiz, in which he writes:

"Your word is the power that you have to create. It is through the word that you manifest everything."

Another favorite book of mine that talks about the power of the word is *The Hidden Messages in Water* by Masaru Emoto. In this book, he takes photographs of water crystals after words are spoken or simply thought into the water. The beautiful words produced beautiful crystals, and the negative words either produced no crystals at all or produced distorted, disturbed-looking crystals. Now take into account that the percentage of water in the average human is around 60%.

Imagine the power the Word has on you.

Words matter...words leave a lasting impression. Words are powerful and, when used correctly, can end wars, inspire a nation, mend hearts, and ignite the next great invention and generation. When misused, they can destroy, tear down, and paralyze us into fear, hate, addiction, and depression. I don't know about you, but if words can leave impressions so deep within us that trigger emotions so strong after a year or even decades after they have been spoken, I'm choosing to use my words wisely, and to be mindful of the words I'm giving my power to and speak to heal, not harm.

You Are Not Your Triggers

Triggers are triggers. You are not a trigger. You may trigger another person, but you are not a trigger. I realize that triggers come in all shapes, sounds, smells, and sizes. Some are so big we won't even dare touch them in this book. But even the biggest and ugliest triggers—the deepest, most scarring, and most debilitating triggers—do not belong to you. Despite the horrific things you may have experienced or had done to you, you are still the same beautiful, loving, deserving, and worthy person. Bad people do bad things, and those that have fallen victim to their attacks need to know that their actions do not determine "your" worth. Place the shame on the one to blame, and you are not it.

No matter the size of your trigger, source, meaning, or context, know that you are not weak for having them, and never feel shame for giving them your power.

Triggers Are Our Teachers

All triggers can be our teachers when we are ready to learn from them. But it takes time, support, and a safe space to process them. Depending on the nature of your trigger, you will know how much support you will need. One thing for certain is that you never process them alone. Swimming in my shame because of my unsafe belief that I am a drama queen only isolates me, separates me, and tricks me into believing that I don't matter; that my case is different and that it's better to keep my secrets safe within me. There is no longer shame in my pain because I am no longer playing this victim.

Labels Do Not Define You

Just as you are not your triggers, you are also not your label. When we give our power to the label we have been given, be it a medical diagnosis or social characterization, we are not it. Our labels may help us better understand a condition we live with, a disability we deal with, or a disease that we carry, but it does not define who we are as a person. When my girlfriend was diagnosed with cancer, she didn't lose who she was because of it. She was still the same intelligent, talented, beautiful, sassy diva that she was before her diagnosis. When I was labeled an alcoholic by a chemical dependency doctor, it didn't take away my soul, purpose, passions, or power. I am only powerless over alcohol if I choose to give it my power. Some might argue that we are all powerless, which may be true, but when we believe in a power greater than ourselves, are we really? All things are possible when I am connected to my power source, which is me, myself, and my Higher Power.

You Are Not a Byproduct

You are not a byproduct of your environment. Don't let anyone tell you differently. Just because you got dealt a crappy hand, grew up in a less-than-desirable neighborhood, or hooked up with some shady characters, that doesn't mean that is who you are and what you deserve. This goes back to Identity Sabotage, not SELF. You tend to believe the lie when a mind virus has corrupted your operating system.

It starts at birth and grows from there. However, it's in the early stages of child development that these mind viruses root. We develop coping mechanisms and armor that create a false sense of who we are. We start acting and showing up as "we see ourselves" and catalog the experience and outcome as proof of our unsafe beliefs. Over time, we change our brains to reinforce these unsafe beliefs and become physically dependent on the emotions, feelings, chemicals, and outcomes they produce. Don't let your past dictate your future.

66 *You can't change the people around you, but you can change the people around you. ~ Joshua Fields Millburn* 99

The second most powerful tool for healing is **forgiveness.**

You can't heal what you don't expose. It was by exposing my wounds instead of trying to cover them up that I could give them the love and attention they needed to heal. One of my favorite quotes (while writing this book, I discovered who wrote it) is from Senator Alan Simpson, who said,

66 Hatred corrodes the container it is carried in. 99

This will be the only time I bring politics into this book, but it is too good not to mention when talking about forgiveness.

When I began to face my pain, I first discovered that the guilt and shame I was carrying weren't mine to hold. Many co-dependents and empaths suffered from this trauma response. I believe it is where my people-pleasing addiction came from. I would hold all the blame and the emotions that should have been felt by the person responsible for it but wasn't. I would internalize it as if I were doing it and then judge what that person should have felt. I would apologize for other people's actions. I would manipulate my environment to mitigate any potential drama from the other person. I would lie, even stay silent, if that meant it would avoid conflict. All of that I carried as if it was mine. But it wasn't. This is what growing up in dysfunction, rejection, and abandonment looks like.

This newfound awareness allowed me to forgive myself for holding onto toxic memories that my body did not deserve to hold. I began to separate myself from the experiences I was exposed to and see them from a different perspective.

I found empathy and compassion for myself and others from this new perspective. I began to understand that hurt people hurt people, not because they don't like or even love you, but because they don't like or love themselves.

The more I forgave, the lighter I felt. The more I let go of my old story, a new one emerged. People say you can't change the past, but I beg to differ. The past rewrites itself when you begin to see things from an enlightened mindset. The moment you begin to let go of your old story is when you start writing a new one. You are the author of your own life; it's a new day to write a new page, not a run-on sentence.

You are absolutely capable of creating the life you can't stop thinking about. It's planted in you for a reason. Life isn't pass or fail. Your past is the teacher and your present is the student. No matter how many times you dropped out or got held back, you can always re-enroll and become the valedictorian.

Embrace the idea that Surrender is the pathway to healing and Forgiveness is the destination. The freedom you will feel and the love for yourself and others you will experience are well worth the journey. You are made for more and have everything you need to succeed within you.

"You had the power to go home all along, Dorothy."

Meditation for Healing

Hands resting on thighs, palms facing up

Today I choose Peace

Today I surrender to things I cannot control

Today I choose Joy

Today I surrender to what I think I know and let it go

Today I release the Past

Today I resolve to live in the Present

Today I am willing and open to receiving solutions

Today I allow obstacles to be removed

Today I choose peace and release all that does not serve my higher good

Today I choose peace and release

Essential Oils to Promote and Support Inner Healing

Palmarosa:

- Reduces Insecurity.
- Lightens Grief.
- Relieves Sadness.
- Invites us to begin a healing process.

Ylang ylang:

- Encourages a Relaxed Attitude.
- Soothes and Inhibits Anger and Frustration.
- Promotes Letting go.

Myrrh:

- Promotes Peace and Tranquility.
- Balances Heart Chakra.
- Overactive Mind.
- Reduces Worry.
- Calms Anxiety.

PART TWO

Disconnect to Reconnect

Stories of Self-Discovery to Recovery

*" We must be willing to let go of the life we planned "
so as to have the life that is awaiting us.*

~ Joseph Campbell

7

It's Not About Self-Sabotage

The core underlining message in this book is about recovering from Identity Sabotage. We have been living a life based on untruths and have adopted these unsafe beliefs as our identity. Looking at our life through new perspective lenses, we can see a new reality based on Truth.

Without these lenses, we see a hard, unfair world determined to restrain us. We view life as a struggle and become victims of an environment we manifest in our minds.

The Matrix Mind is where Ego wants us to live. The always-striving yet never-arriving mentality deprives us of joy, gratitude, and fulfillment in life. We live only in the past while fearing our future, never living in the present.

We consume, compete, and compare while never measuring up to the Matrix Mind of more.

Should have, would have, could have become our mantra.

I "should" have done this.

I "could" have done that.

If only they "would" have done this.

We compete instead of compliment. We compare instead of connect. We consume instead of being content.

Our identity has been sabotaged by Ego. The Ego is fueled by doubt, leaving us with a self-worth deficiency. This deficiency begins to crave what the Ego seeks, and we become addicted to feeding it.

Our "True Self" resources have been stripped, leaving us deprived. Just as cancer feeds on sugar, the Ego feeds on fear. The more we give it, the stronger it gets. Saying we "Self-Sabotage" is eating at Willy Wonka's Chocolate Factory. Self-Sabotage is the secret ingredient.

To better understand Identity Sabotage, we must first understand the Ego. My favorite definition of Ego is from Wayne Dyer.

EGO = Edging God Out

Having a spiritual connection is the breath of life. To breathe in this power greater than yourself gives you life. Many people struggle with this power being "God." It may be from past experiences, religion, or what you've been fed to believe. All I know is that the planet was made for us to thrive. This world's natural forces and resources work with us and through us. The same force that makes the Earth rotate and the tides of the ocean turn are also working for you.

If you struggle to find a higher power, I encourage you to meditate on something Matthew Perry said in his interview with Diane Sawyer. Paraphrasing, "If you think we are the power, try making a wave stop or a plant." Forget trying to make it grow; can you make the plant? The energy of Mother Nature is a power greater than you. Trees taller and more powerful than you provide the oxygen you breathe as you give the carbon dioxide it needs.

When we are in flow with source energy, we are all one.

The Ego speaks the loudest when it feels threatened. Removing the Truth is the only way it can continue living its Lie. God is Truth. By removing God, we become spiritually bankrupt and desperate, leaving us susceptible to sabotage.

We cling to whatever gives us power, even if that power drains us.

Ego is that power.

The Ego takes on many forms and wears many hats.

Jealousy: The belief that we are to have all we desire. We become jealous of those who have more of what we think we deserve. This emotion separates us from our Truth and each other.

Pride: A disconnect to spiritual growth that prevents us from sharing.

Envy: Reinforced unsafe beliefs that if we don't measure up to the ones we set our bar to, we are not as worthy as they are.

Hate: The fuel that feeds envy.

Fear: A measuring stick of our worth provided to us by the Ego.

Doubt: Reinforced unsafe beliefs on the measuring stick of fear.

Victim: The house where Ego lives and wants us to unpack. The longer we live there, the more mail we get saying we belong. Victimhood becomes our new address.

Greed: The Matrix Mind's highway to hell.

Righteousness: The need to prove our dominance over others, believing this power gives us worth.

Unworthiness: The landlord to victimhood.

Symptoms of Ego

- We confuse Ego with confidence, ending up conceded.
- We play God.
- We believe we know best and have all the power to control or manipulate people, places, and things.
- Discrimination.
- Isolation.
- Alienation.

Side Effects of EGO

- We feel lost, alone, and without purpose.
- We see ourselves as victims.
- Burnout.
- Depression.
- Anxiety.
- Addiction.
- Feelings of deficiency.

To say we self-sabotage implies we know ourselves. But if we knew who we were, we would know we are incapable of sabotage.

Self-Sabotage is the **CEO** of the **EGO**.

Creating Ego Overflow

It will stop at nothing to provide enough evidence to prove you are either better than or less than. Its only job is to create a surplus of resources to supply the demands set by the Ego.

Where our Soul-Self says: *I am not more than or less than anyone. I simply am.*

You were born for a reason. You have a purpose. Everything on this planet serves a purpose, including YOU. We are all a part of this magnificent world specifically designed with unique talents, gifts, and messages to share. Who are we to say which one is more valuable than the other? As a collective, we are all equally vital to the Universal Mission.

What is The Mission?

As spiritual beings having a human experience, each mission is exclusive to the person having the experience. That being said, the purpose is to evolve through love.

You were perfectly created with everything you needed to grow. The Universe provides all the ingredients to nurture and promote your transformation. With its power, it supports you. Every breath you take from source energy brings life to your purpose.

How do you breathe in source energy?

Meditation is the pathway to peace and a direct line of communication to source energy. Set the intention on your breathing to connect while envisioning its presence surrounding you. Every mindful inhale fills your soul with this divine presence expelling the Ego on the exhale.

Picture loving white light entering your body as the heavy darkness leaves it on the out-breath.

While continuing this visual breathing exercise, begin to repeat this mantra.

> *Heal what is broken.*
>
> *Restore what is forgotten.*
>
> *Awaken my power within.*

The more you practice this technique, the lighter you will start to feel. This cleansing exercise promotes balance and restores clarity. The more aligned we become, the easier it is to connect and stay connected.

Throughout the day, you may notice a shift occurring, pulling you back to your Ego's will. When this happens, pause, breathe, and repeat; *I realign with you in mind.* This will break up the static trying to disconnect you and bring you back into alignment with source energy.

The next time you feel your Ego trying to sabotage your identity, repeat the visual breathing meditation and mantra. You'll soon discover the power it once had over you weakens as your Truth breaks through.

The past stays in the past, and the future reveals itself in its proper time as we ground ourselves in the present, receiving its gifts.

These gifts come in all different forms and experiences and can only be acquired in the present. Although you may not open all the gifts immediately, you will begin to see why they were given to you when the time is right.

STORYTIME

Sitting in my car, full of fear for what I was about to walk into, I slowly found my way to the door. I was a single mom with two children, soon to be twice divorced. And I was about to open the door to our new home for the first time.

Just a few months earlier I was crying in the living room, feeling sorry for myself that my three-month marriage was over. The kids were at their dad's, and I was alone once again. However, I was never by myself. I always had my new best friend, Chardonnay, by my side. She came into my life in my late 20s and had a unique way of making me feel safe. As we sat together in that living room, I tried to make my own; I felt a peace come over me.

Up to this point, I was barely surviving. But thanks to denial, I could not see it. I didn't own the house I tried to make my home; it belonged to my estranged husband. While drinking my wine and listening to music, which is disguised as your companion but really just encourages self-pity, much like my new best friend (Chardonnay, weren't you listening?), I felt calm. I knew I had to make a move, but felt powerless over *how*.

This calm was not the same calm I would feel three glasses in; this calm was peace. I stopped writing in my journal, which was now covered in smeared ink from my toxic tears, and began to pray. Desperate to escape the misery I was drowning in, I asked God for help. The background noise faded as my awareness focused on the energy filling the room. This energy whispered to me, "Buy your own damn house."

What a crazy thought to entertain. How could I buy my own home? What sick joke is the Universe trying to play? Did they not know who I was? I was a single mother with two children working a job that barely paid the bills. My credit was shot and I had no savings. I was pretty sure this idea of me buying a home was just another delusional daydream and not part of my plan anytime soon, if ever!

Except as I cried myself to sleep that night, the idea of having a home of my own grew stronger. Suddenly that crazy idea didn't sound so crazy. Despite what my Ego was trying to tell me, I decided to call my girlfriend, who just happened to be a real estate agent. I told her my insane idea of buying my own home, expecting her to agree. But she didn't. She thought it was a brilliant idea and wondered what had taken me so long.

Hurdle after hurdler was cleared with plenty of room to spare, and before I knew it, I was pre-approved for my own home loan. One of the biggest hurdles was my source of income. Shortly after deciding to shoot for the moon, I was promoted with a salary made for two. The down payment came from a few unlikely sources that appeared out of thin air. And my credit score was just where it needed to be to approve that loan. It was like the Universe was giving me the house.

Oh yes, the house, we need to *find* the house. Determined to keep my kids in the same school, my search was limited to a specific zip code. And after a few searches, we found her. She was perfect! Not too big, not too small, and exactly the price point I needed. We put in the offer and it was immediately accepted. One step closer!

Then the day came when I was invited to sign my life away, and I panicked. My heart was racing, fueled with fear. This was where the truth would all come out. I was an imposter. I could see my future flashing before my eyes while I waited for the loan officer to tell me the gig was up. But she didn't. I thought at least I can put off telling my kids that the rooms they picked out will not be theirs to unpack for another day.

But that day never came.

There I was, sitting in my car with the actual keys to that house. *My* house. Walking up to the front porch, fear flooded my mind with doubt. I still couldn't believe they had let me walk off with the keys. Yet there I was, about to unlock the door to my dreams.

I walked through that house as an owner, not a guest, yet every day I felt like an intruder. Sure, I painted the walls and decorated the house with family photos and cute signs that said, *Blessed, Home Sweet Home*, and *Welcome*, but deep down inside, I knew it wouldn't last.

My Ego was hard-wired to struggle. My self-worth deficiency began to crave what my Ego sought, and I was addicted to feeding it. That was all I ever knew. It was comfortable, it was safe, and *that* was my one true home.

Little by little, my actions began to match my unsafe beliefs once again. My drinking increased, my work performance declined, and almost all of my relationships fell stagnant. I wanted nothing more than to have what was right in front of me. To say I SELF-SABOTAGED what I desperately sought and fought for is a LIE. My Authentic Self, my Soul-Self, manifested itself into what my Ego Self was trying to take away.

My true identity was stolen and replaced with an imposter committing fraud daily. I quit my job before I could lose it and fell behind on my mortgage payments. Every fraudulent transaction bought me a false sense of security that reinforced my unsafe beliefs. With my true self hijacked, I was subconsciously attempting to ensure I failed to allow another alibi as proof of my erroneous beliefs.

However, the Universe had other plans. When our free will wanders off too far from home, our Higher Power will step in to alter our course. Fortunately it does not present itself with neon flashing lights saying *turn here*. Most times, it's a dead end or flat tire that stops us in our tracks. Yes, fortunately! We grow through what we go through. Therefore, the Universe will not always give us a free hand-up. Unlike the hand-up it gave me to buy my home, this time, it would make me fight to keep it.

Realizing my own Ego's demise, I began to reflect on all the events that led me to own the keys that opened that door. Thankfully just because our identity has been sabotaged doesn't mean our Soul-Self is dead. I could tap into my inner intelligence long enough to see where I had veered off course. I became a spectator to the S*!t Show I was once again trying to manifest into reality. My actions mirrored someone I knew I was not. My Soul-Self and Ego-Self were at war!

When we awaken to our Truth, we will stop at nothing to redeem it.

The Truth and the Lie were exposed.

Truth: *I deserved that home and the right to call it my own.*

versus

Lie: *I am unworthy because of the things I have done. I don't deserve to be happy.*

I had two choices:

Eat the Banana or Die.

Like any addiction, it only has power over us when we choose to give it our power.

And my self-worth deficiency was about to be restored. The less I fed the Ego what it craved, the stronger I became.

I am not a victim of my circumstances, regardless of who and how they were created. I survived 100% of the time my Ego tried to take me out. My track record was all the proof I needed.

I chose to eat the Banana.

I reached out for help and, once again, the Shift Shapers appeared. Of course, you still have to do the hard work and heavy lifting. It's not a free ride, but it is a joy ride when you suit up and show up. And maybe buckle up, as it can get a little bumpy.

Recovery from Identity Sabotage does not give you a free pass, either. You will have to eat lots of humble pie, right wrongs, and clean up your side of the street regardless. It gives you the power to move ahead with purpose and humility.

Asking for help can be one of the hardest things to do when our identity has been sabotaged by the Ego. Our unsafe belief that we must never show weakness or vulnerability only blocks us from our Truth. When we let go of the Ego and surrender to Humility, we find strength and solutions.

It was in admitting my wrongs that they were made right. I was given a clear pathway to move forward with grace and humble pride.

There is nothing wrong with having pride in your work accomplishments or sharing stories of your growth and promotions. Celebrating our successes and experiences is what makes life enjoyable and connecting meaningful.

Sharing is caring when you are sharing for the right reasons. The Ego speaks to "be seen" and listens to talk, whereas our Truth speaks to "feel seen" and listens to understand. People enjoy hearing about our accomplishments because they know how much we care. When we lead with love and push pride aside, our stories lift others up, not tear them down.

I've learned that your home is where you decide to reside and root. It's not a status symbol or an asset. Nor is your job, title, or bank account. I eventually moved out of that house, renting it to some wonderful families to create their own memories while I made new ones where I live today.

You are an asset, and your value is priceless.

Meditation for "Letting Go" of the Ego

Hands resting on thighs, Palms facing up.

Breathe in deeply and exhale completely.

Repeat each line three times out loud or in your head.

I Surrender

I Surrender to everything I think I know about who I am

I Surrender to my Ego and Let it Go

I Surrender to my resistance and Let it Go

I Surrender to my weakness, for here I find my Strength

I Surrender to my fear, for here I find my Faith

I Surrender to everything I think I know and Embrace WHO I AM

Essential Oils for Letting Go

Bergamot:

- Known to Reduce Anger.
- Calm Anxiety.
- Reduce Loneliness.
- Quite Fear.
- Lessen Insecurity.

Frankincense:

- Known to Promote the Tranquility of the Mind.
- Removes Negative Thinking and Emotions.
- Reduces Bad Memories and Thoughts of the Past.
- Dispels Depression, Stress, and Anxiety

For more guided meditations, visit: www.soulshacksisters.com

And visit me on Insight Timer @Tonya De'laine

8

It's Not About the Banana

Before we peel back on this book's title chapter, I should preface it by saying that reason alone made this one of the hardest to write. Finding the words to paint a picture that would capture that "*aha*" moment wasn't as easy as I thought. The feelings and emotions came flooding back, but the words were harder to find. It honestly reminded me of the Maya Angelou quote:

> *I've learned that people will forget what you said, people will forget what you did, but people will never forget how you made them feel.*

It has been more than 15 years since that day, and once I sat down to write about how that one argument changed the way I looked at life, all the "feels" came flooding back, but the words... for those I had to do a little digging. This is important to mention because words are powerful, and we must be mindful of what words we attach to our emotions. Emotions reflect our past and what we are now feeling in the present.

So, I peeled back that old rotten Banana for the sake of this book, opened some Brené Brown books to help find the right words to match my emotions, and got to work.

Here is how it all began...

STORYTIME

My daughter was sitting at the breakfast counter, ready for another exciting day in second grade. Her beautiful big brown eyes and adorable new bob haircut were staring at me with a sleepy yet excited look while I poured her cereal. Little did I know that within the next 30 minutes, I was about to embark on a groundbreaking revelation that is the basis of this book and, of course, its title.

Picture a banana lying on the kitchen counter, a perfectly ripe yellow banana. Of course, like any other good mother, I peeled that banana and cut it into my daughter's cereal. What seemed like a simple and easy choice to me turned out to be the game-changer for my partner. Just as my daughter put the spoon up to her mouth to take that first yummy bite, he entered the kitchen asking, with a slightly irritated tone (and that infamous vein protruding from his forehead), *"Where's my banana?"*

Confused, as I hadn't seen him in the kitchen until then, I responded, "What banana?"

"The banana that I put right here," he said, as he aggressively pointed down to the counter, hitting it with his index finger with to emphasize every word, "THAT. I. PUT. RIGHT. HERE!"

"Oh, I'm sorry," I said. "I didn't realize that was 'your' banana. I used it for her cereal."

"That was MY BANANA," he shouted back at me again.

It reminded me of that episode on *Friends*, when Ross lost his mind over someone taking his sandwich. (Man, that was such a great show...)

"MY SANDWICH?!? MMMYYYY SANDWICH!!!!!!"

At this point, my daughter's mouth was wide open in mid-bite, unsure if she should eat her breakfast or piece the banana back together as if nothing had happened, all while my voice began to rise out of frustration and utter embarrassment. I was beyond upset; I was furious! How could a grown-ass man throw such a hissy fit over a stupid banana? How dare he act like he was more important than anyone else in the house to declare that it was **HIS** banana. I told him to calm down and stop making it such a big deal.

Of course, telling someone to calm down never makes them calm down. I've heard it said that if you tell a woman to calm down, you better duck. Well, let me tell you, telling him to calm down was no different; he lost it! I lost it!

THIS WOULD HAVE BEEN THE PERFECT TIME TO PAUSE

Having not yet developed my 5-Step Method, I knew it was best to walk away and calm down before I made matters worse.

As I stomped up the stairs (yes, I was having my own hissy fit at this point), I yelled, "I can't believe you are acting like this over a stupid banana!" And then came the famous last words...

"IT'S NOT ABOUT THE BANANA!" he shouted back.

I didn't say another word; I couldn't if I wanted to. I was speechless, puzzled, and stunned. *It's not about the banana?* What does he mean "It's not about the banana?" Was he not in the kitchen with me, arguing about how I took his banana? Did he not embarrass his step-daughter and me about his banana? I did my best to collect myself, smile, and take my daughter and son (who luckily was in the shower while "Bananagate" broke and didn't hear a thing) to school. All I could think about the rest of the day was that fight and the final words spoken...

It's NOT about the BANANA.

Well then, what the hell was it about? What happened the night before that would make a man lose his mind over a freaking BANANA? What made him so mad that missing his morning banana could cause such a scene? Instantly, I go to that famous "woman's well" of "Is it about ME?" (LADIES...Why do we do this to ourselves? Why do we feel that if something is wrong, it must be because of something WE did or didn't do?)

Did I do or say something wrong?

Is he not attracted to me anymore?

I should have made sure we had more bananas in the house.

I'll make sure to get more on the way home and text him a cute message with a picture of a bunch of bananas saying, "I love you bunches."

And on and on I went. Talk about being a people-pleasing, co-dependent empath. I went straight into fix-it mode and took the blame and shame as my own to try and make my environment feel better.

But was it?

Who was "better" now that there were bananas back in the house?

Let me tell you... NO ONE! Well, maybe the banana growers, but seriously, that's just pushing it.

The minute we start reacting to someone else's "acting," we lose our Truth in the process.

We begin to believe their story as our own and show up for the part.

Except, **IT'S NOT OUR PART TO PLAY!**

PAUSE

When *someone else* overreacts to a situation, it is almost ALWAYS about the other person and what they are going through. Their emotions, perceptions, and perspectives at that moment are NOT your reality; it's theirs. *(This includes you, too, sorry, not sorry.)*

We can't be held responsible or blamed for other people's thoughts and feelings (or doings, for that matter). Thoughts and feelings that arose from their past experiences that led up to that one moment that broke the floodgates DO NOT BELONG TO YOU unless you allow it.

Naturally, we as humans want to blame others for why we feel a certain way. We want to believe that it is never *our* fault that something is happening to us that makes us feel cheated or mistreated. It's much easier to point the finger, yell, and put someone else down than to **PAUSE**, look at ourselves at that moment, and ask ourselves **WHY** are we so upset over a BANANA?

Unfortunately, most people will never *PAUSE, PEEL, REVEAL, and HEAL* from what holds them back or causes them to overreact, but luckily you are not one of those people. You bought this book and, hopefully, have started to see the tools and ways you can peel back the Bananas in your life and the lives of others around you to reveal the unsafe beliefs that hold you back from the lies you tell yourself.

Today you can start taking responsibility for your own Bananas and toss out the rotten ones that don't belong to you or no longer serve you. Or you can make Banana Bread (I have a fantastic recipe at the end of this book).

Now let's rewind this story and use my **5-Step Method**.

This method will help you discover what lies you are telling yourself in all areas of your life and reveal the unsafe beliefs that are holding you back and preventing you from living your best life.

PEEL

"IT'S NOT ABOUT THE BANANA." Still stewing, dwelling, and repeating it in my head, and I'm sure out loud, I did what any average 30-something woman would do—I called my girlfriends for a "meeting" (a.k.a. "meet at the local wine bar"). Looking back at it now, this is not a productive way to deal with your problems. Talking it out, yes; having to consume alcohol to do it, not so much.

However, at this point in my journey, that was what I did, again and again. And again. So, there we were, rehashing that moment when life stood still, and all I could do was replay it over and over while listening to my YaYas share their stories and thoughts about the meaning of that food fight.

"It's NOT about the Banana!"

After we tore him apart for being a pathetic excuse for a man, we could all agree that this was not about that banana and was more about him not feeling secure with himself. This insecurity had prevented him from being fully present or available to me and the kids.

He was living in a world centered around HIM and HIM alone.

WOW! Big INHALE, big EXHALE.

He was fighting some powerful dragons that needed to be slain, and the banana was the deflector.

REVEAL

The *Banana* had been peeled, and boy, did it reveal an ugly but honest Truth. Without divulging too much more about my ex-husband's back story, as it is not mine to tell, I will say this was spot on. Why didn't I see it before?

I had plenty of opportunities to see it. How could I have allowed myself to live in an environment, or, worse yet, put my kids in one that was not fully accepting and loving?

Most times, when peeling back other people's layers, you expose your Truths more than you do their own.

> *Spot Check and Full Disclaimer, if you spot it, you got it!*
>
> *It's always a good idea to take a long, hard look in the mirror and ask yourself if you feel or think the same way. Most times, the answer is Yes, because what we see in others is usually what we fear in ourselves.*

I can't tell you how many times someone has irritated me for being selfish and inconsiderate of my time, only to realize later on that I was feeling this way because I was being selfish and inconsiderate of their time. Both parties are valuable. Who am I to say mine is more important?

Not knowing this at the time, I could see his part in it, and that was enough to let it go. I hurt for him and, to this day, pray that he has finally found the ability to love himself so that he can give and receive the love he deserves completely.

Now that I let the banana go, I could move on with my life, which is precisely what I did. Because I didn't do a proper spot check and own my part, I could pretend everything was okay, convince myself he was the one with the issues, and move on.

This not-so-healthy relationship continued off and on for another few years with new and some not-so-new arguments, more "meetings with my Yayas" followed by more arguments and more "meetings."

Until he secretly moved out one day in July while the kids were at their dad's and I was at work.

I'll never forget *that* day either, and I'm embarrassed to say that this wasn't the first time.

But it was the last.

I called him from work to see if he wanted to take the kids out that night to get fireworks, as the 4th of July was just around the corner. My call didn't go through, so I called again. Same problem. I called again and again, but it still wouldn't go through. I tried sending a text message, but it failed to send. I tried it again, and it failed again. I tried calling my office to see if it was my phone, and the call went through with no problem. So I tried to call him again. Nothing.

I texted my girlfriend and she replied right away. What the heck is wrong with his phone, I thought to myself. Maybe it was the cell towers, or it had been shut off by mistake. But it's his work phone; how could that be?

I know... I will email him and tell him that his phone is dead. What a brilliant idea! So I emailed him, telling him that I tried calling and texting, and it wasn't going through. He responded instantly, "Your calls and texts aren't going through because I blocked you. I moved out. I'm done."

Ummmm, excuse me? You blocked me?

WOW, this was a new level of a messed-up banana split. I have never loved that Gwen Stephani song more.

> This S*!t is Bananas,
> B. A. N. A. N. A. S.

But seriously, he BLOCKED me, moved out all his stuff, and was done? The inner voice I heard loud and clear was, *"You Get What You Tolerate."* The fact was I didn't love and respect myself enough to know that I wasn't being treated with respect; I didn't love myself enough to know I was not being appreciated; and I didn't love myself enough to let him go.

One of my dear friends once said to me, *"Go where you are celebrated, not tolerated!"* I wish those wise words hit me then like they do today. The teacher appears when the student is ready, *right*? If I had taken that long, hard look in the mirror that night, and came to the realization that he didn't love himself enough to love me, I might have also been able to accept that I didn't love myself much either.

I could not appreciate love because I didn't believe I was worthy of it. Had I been able to see this Truth, I would have been the one to end it long before. It takes what it takes, and for me on that day, it took him blocking me to finally see that I was stuck in a toxic habit loop, void of emotions, love, boundaries, and respect for self and others.

I was battered, abused, lost, and sick. I needed help. I needed clarity. I needed hope. But instead, I ran, numbed, and avoided the Banana for another five years.

That was my way of coping! RUN! AVOID! DENY! PRETEND!

You can only run for so long before the weight you are running from slows you down to a complete STOP, runs you over like a midnight train to Georgia filled with oil, spills all over you, catches on fire, and burns for another five years. This was the Truth I had been avoiding up to this point. I was so determined not to let life get the best of me that I continued to act as if it hadn't.

HEAL

Instead, I had been living in denial. I had been living other people's lies, trying to make them fit into my story. The Truth was it didn't fit because it wasn't meant to. The lies that I wasn't worthy of love, commitment, or honesty that I believed was truth kept me coming back for more. I forced it, distorted it, and made it look as pretty as possible, hoping it would resemble something close to what I had dreamed of as a child.

By embracing the uncomfortable and allowing yourself to see the Truth, you give yourself permission to finally become comfortable. This is how you heal from the hurt. As much as it may pain you to read this, you have to FEEL it, just enough to HEAL it. I want to empathize "enough" because we can lose ourselves in the feelings that come up when we look in the rearview mirror.

We must remind ourselves that the past is the past, and we only need to revisit it when we need to move away from it. When we hold up camp in the past, we prevent ourselves from healing in the present. We must feel it just enough to know the meaning behind the healing and use that wisdom to move forward. That is precisely what I did.

I began to see the patterns in all areas of my life and how I relived the past in the present every single day. I knew that if I wanted things to be different, *I* had to be different. I had to think differently, I had to see things differently, and I had to allow myself to experience new experiences in order to feel differently.

> **❝** *If you keep doing what you're doing, you'll keep getting what* **❞**
> *you're getting.*
>
> *~ Quote by someone cool*

The Truth was that our relationship was toxic long before the banana made us split. I just didn't want to see it. Instead, I played the victim in the relationship I kept showing up for. My unsafe beliefs around love and relationships caused me to seek out people and experiences that would validate them. The more evidence I had to prove my erroneous belief system, the truer it became and the more validated I felt in believing it.

But now, the Truth and the Lie were exposed, and I had a crucial choice to make,

Eat the Banana or Die.

The banana exposed the Truth, and I could either accept it and allow myself a new experience to change, or I could ignore it and continue living the way I was while slowly dying inside.

I chose to Eat the Banana.

And I wrote this book!

9

It's Not About the Juice Box

Okay, the title of this chapter can be a little misleading. I'm not talking about your kid's juice box you forgot to pack in their lunch. I'm referring to the grown-up version juice box, otherwise coined "Mommy Juice." For some, this chapter might be right up your alley as you immediately know what I am talking about. For others, not so much.

Maybe it wasn't a juice box for you, but it was a bag of candy, a sleeve of cookies, an entire tub of ice cream, or one more hit on the bong, slot machine, or credit card for those new pair of shoes you just *had* to have. Whatever it was for you, it was an addiction. A way to run, avoid, or fill the big gaping hole that sits in your chest. The one that leaves you feeling crunchy and full of anxiety at the thought of either having nothing to do or being alone, caught off guard by your thoughts. Whatever the reason and whatever the drug of choice, I'm here to tell you that...

YOU ARE NOT ALONE!

What started as a casual drink here, or a few too many drinks there, turned into a full-blown WTF-just-happened moment in my life. I was nearly kicked out of my home. My kids were not sure what had happened to their mom. Friends, family, and employers were left scratching their heads in disbelief, trying to rectify the woman they once knew with the woman I had become, full of emptiness and despair.

You see, I wasn't always a Juice Box Mom. I was a hard-working, goal-driven, PTA-chairing, best-friend sharing, momma-bear-caring woman who had a vision of peace, love, and happiness for all. Growing up in a single-family home with a mom who struggled to get by, I vowed never to do the same.

I wanted nothing more than to graduate, move away, and make a name for myself. Success was the only way I could see my way out and the only thing I felt I had control of. How that looked and how I got there didn't matter, as long as it meant I didn't have to live in a trailer park on food stamps. My dreams were big, and my heart and passion for life were bigger. Even though I never truly felt like I belonged anywhere, I knew deep down inside that it for sure wasn't where I was.

STORYTIME

The second I graduated high school, I was promoted to store manager of a men's clothing line in Seattle, Washington. My dreams of becoming a fashion buyer for Nordstrom were well on their way. Of course, I still held out hope that I would be discovered by some big-shot Hollywood producer and land a starring role in a blockbuster franchise. Again, I've always dreamed big, as it was my way to escape my reality growing up. Secretly, a part of me still holds on to that dream of meeting Jordan Knight from the New Kids on the Block one day, so yeah.... Never give up on your dreams, kids!

At the ripe old age of 18, I was moving to the big city and leaving the small town behind me in my rearview mirror. I finally felt free to spread my wings and be me, even though, looking back, I had no clue as to what "being me" was.

But one thing I have now come to learn is that no matter where you go, there you are.

Of course, at 18, I hadn't seen how the patterns of denial, shame, regret, or habitual bad decision-making was leading to this not ending well. And trust me, there was already enough evidence to back it; I was just too naïve to see it. Plus, drinking was never an issue with me. I didn't do drugs, and I hardly drank alcohol. I had no time for them, and they for sure did not serve me and my vision for my future life. I was going places!

I had my very own studio apartment in downtown Seattle. The Space Needle was my playground as I would walk up to the Seattle Center every day to hop on the monorail to work at the Westlake Mall. Those were the days! Celebrities would come into my store almost weekly to the point that I created an autograph wall behind our register to capture it all. I was setting up window displays for the mall, merchandising the store, and dreaming of becoming a fashion buyer for Nordstrom, which was just down the block. I would go in there daily and walk around, pretending to be the buyer for this line or that line, staring at all the amazingly beautiful and tall people that worked there. They had style and a presence that was intimidating yet exciting. I couldn't believe that this was my life. I LOVED it. I made amazing friends from all different backgrounds, and finally started to feel like I had found my people. I even had a professional headshot and portfolio and went out on a few auditions. I was living my best life.

Then a curve ball.... My father, whom I barely had a relationship with, yet so desperately wanted to be like because he was highly successful, said to me, "When are you going to get a real job?"

When am I going to get a real job? I couldn't believe what I was hearing! I *had* a real job. Didn't I? Well, I thought I did until that moment. Then I began to question everything, including myself and my life decisions.

> *Don't allow the uncertainty in others to cause you to doubt the certainty in you!*

You see, growing up, it was just my mom and me. My dad wasn't really in the picture. He lived in the city and we lived in a small farm town several hours away. I didn't even know I had a father until I was in fourth grade, when he started to pop in and out of my life. At first, I didn't know what to think or feel. I didn't even know what feelings were, let alone have the words to describe them. If I had to come up with some words today to describe this awkward experience, I would say I felt stressed, with a mixture of overwhelmed and a little sprinkle of anxiety (shout out to Brené Brown for helping me find the words today to explain my emotions).

When he would come to pick me up to stay with him for the weekend, hours away from everything I knew, I felt so uncomfortable, out of place, and alone. Looking back now, I wonder how *he* must have felt picking up his nine-year-old daughter in a not-so-desirable neighborhood surrounded by some questionable characters. It's no wonder he later asked me *when I was going to get a real job.* He didn't understand my vision; granted I didn't share it with him, but he didn't know anything other than what *he* was doing. Success was all he knew, and striving for it every day kept him disconnected from me and the reality he left me in.

As years passed, he continued to play a role in my life and eventually helped me in more ways than I ever realized. It wasn't until long after his premature passing that I was able to really *see* him.

He was doing the best he could with what he had. His inability to love completely was a direct result of not loving himself. Nothing I did or didn't do in my early adult years would ever change that. I could "look" the part. I could "fit in" with the corporate world. I could get married, have children, buy a house, and climb the corporate ladder, but nothing I did would ever open his heart to loving himself.

I learned that we will always come up short when we seek validation, acceptance, and love from others to make ourselves feel seen. You can't give what you don't have, nor can you look to others to give it to you. It's an inside job!

Nonetheless, this lesson wasn't learned until much, much, much later in my self-healing journey.

After my father's passing, I faced more disappointment, rejection, doubt, fear, and—at the top of the list—RESENTMENT. I resented my father for asking me "*When are you going to get a real job?*" And was even more resentful for the fact that I *listened to him* and left my dreams to go into property management. I resented that he left me and his two grandkids with nothing—knowing we were young and struggling with a premature baby and more than $100,000 in medical bills, he left us with nothing. For the next 25 years I worked in an industry that, at best, paid the bills, and at worst, slowly killed my Soul.

Did someone say **"Project" Emotional Response?** Pretty sure if you look it up in the dictionary, you'll see my face!

This was the twisted mindset that would eventually catch up to me drinking juice boxes out of the closet, but I still have more of a picture to paint before I take you to that happy destination of self-destruction. I say happy to be funny, but in all honestly, looking back on it now, it was that self-destruction—that total break in my mind, body, and spirit—that SAVED MY LIFE, leading me down that happy trail of destiny.

As time passed, this resentment turned to anger, which turned into a decade of avoiding myself and running on self-will, self-reliance, ambition, Marlboros, and wine, eventually leading me straight into a mental hospital.

One day as I sat in my house with my two babies while my husband was at work, I couldn't help but shake this feeling that life wasn't playing fair, something was missing, and this wasn't how my story was going to end. At this point, I hadn't discovered wine yet, but I had found this thing inside me that had been buried deep down for years. It started to ignite and burn at a slow simmer. Something that told me I was made for more and needed to get back to living my life. I have now realized that some of these emotions I was experiencing were "postpartum depression" mixed with ambition and a genetic disease called alcoholism. Not the best combination, just FYI, but I was off and running before I knew better.

I left my husband, sold our house, and moved from apartment to apartment and relationship after toxic relationship without skipping a beat. What's that old song called? *Looking for love in all the wrong places?* Yeah, that was me. I was looking outside to find peace inside. NEWS FLASH, it doesn't work that way.

I spent the next 10 years job hopping but justifying it in my head that it was in the same industry, so it didn't count, trading spaces like it was a new TV reality show and discovering this magic juice that made me feel like it was all going to be okay. I was living a life of chaos, somehow managing to get by, even if it was by a thin thread of dental floss.

It's funny how you lower your bar without even realizing it, and before you know it, you are a shell of the person you once knew. I remember sitting in my garage one night with my YaYas, drinking wine while crying about how screwed up my life was. At this point, I was in an on-again-off-again relationship that lasted for a decade. (Yes, the Banana guy.) We even got married at one point, which lasted maybe three months before he took off again.

My life was becoming something eligible for the Jerry Springer Show. It was RIDICULOUS. Yet, there I was in denial, justifying it by saying, *look at me, I have a job, just bought my own home, my kids are active in sports, and I even bake cookies. I'm FINE!* Sure, things on the outside looked like I was FINE, but what was happening inside me was anything but.

Redirect Emotional Response at its best!

Before I knew it, the evening wine beacon became a daily occurrence with or without my YaYas. I was making concession after concession in my life that left me financially and spiritually bankrupt. Thank God, I still had some sanity left to finally END the joke of a relationship and embark on a new ME!

I went straight from Redirect to Deflect without skipping a beat! I started another side business—spray tanning clients out of my home—as being an entrepreneur was something I was wired for. However, the one downfall of this is that if we are not spiritually fit and are running from ourselves, this can be a slippery slope. And it was for me. I slipped and fell hard on my butt as I drank around the clock, celebrated my new life, and daydreamed about my future.

I was living a life of denial that was flowing through my backyard. I wish I could tell you that after almost losing my home, kids, and self, I finally put the cork in the wine bottle, but that would be a lie. Did I hear Maury Povich?

When I say, "It's not about the Juice box," I mean it from the depths of my Soul. Alcohol is only a solution until it isn't. Alcohol was fun until it wasn't. Alcohol is your best friend until it takes everything you have ever cared for away from you while telling you it's them, not YOU. For me, the battle with the bottle lasted another four years. In and out of treatment, I tried to fight it, I wanted to beat it, and I tried to prove to the world and all the haters that wanted to use my disease against me that I would win!

IT'S NOT ABOUT THE JUICE BOX.

When your PRIDE is BIGGER than your Circumstance, You'll Never Advance.

Humility is KEY to your prosperity in life. In order for me to *do* better, I had to *be* better. And for me to *be* better, I had to *know* better. For me, knowing better was to walk through that S*!t Storm of life *I* had created, not anyone else. I had to sit in my S*!t long enough to know that I was in it and to understand why I was in it, but not long enough that I smelled like it.

I had to sit in the DIM and FEEL the FEELINGS I had been avoiding with family, men, jobs, hobbies, new businesses, and WINE. I had to peel back that Banana and look at the ROOT cause of my destructive symptoms if I was ever going to recover from them.

In this dim, the Truth and the Lie were exposed.

Truth: *I am deserving of unconditional love even when I get hurt or cause hurt.*

versus

Lie: *People should never hurt me.*

I had two choices:

Eat the Banana or Die.

The leveling of your pride can be painful for anyone with an EGO complex, and boy, did I have one. After spending my entire life trying to PROVE myself to the world, I lost myself in the process. It wasn't until I completely fell apart that I could look at myself for the first time and slowly piece myself back together, one day at a time.

You see, if it wasn't for my dad showing up the way he did in my life, I might not have seen the patterns in my own. If it wasn't for my mom fighting every day to be the amazing human she was and still is, I might not have had the courage and vulnerability to do the same.

To judge them is to judge me. To see them is to see me. The pain and shame I held, they held too. Some were mine, some were theirs, but none were ours to hold. When we keep our Truth hidden, we hold more than secrets; we withhold ourselves from love.

I ate the Banana!

Today I have nothing but love for all that have hurt me, for I know they were hurting, too.

Some people you love so much that you stay away from them, while others you share a Banana with!

It was never about the Juice Box!

10

It's Not About the Marlboros

I love smoking! There I said it.

I loved the social aspect of smoking, taking a smoke break with co-workers to talk about real-life office politics or during a commercial break in a football game or girls' wine night. I loved being able to use it as an excuse; to take a break and go smoke to escape from whatever it was in that moment that was causing me anxiety. Heck, sometimes I just smoked because I wanted to take a mental break and play Pet Rescue Saga or, let's be honest, scroll TikTok (@yogitonya) on my phone instead of crunching out another budget/financial report for work.

Yes, I know. *Redirect Emotional Response*!

Smoking became part of my identity. I knew I shouldn't smoke for obvious health reasons and that it didn't match the message I was trying to send, but for some reason, I was okay with it.

As a little girl, I remember trying to hide my mom's Vantage 100s from her, thinking that would do the trick to make her stop smoking, and it worked... for like 30 minutes. Then she would be frantically pacing the house trying to find them, only to look at me and know I had hidden them. Apparently, I wear my emotions on my sleeve, and my face was a dead giveaway. Of course, to avoid imprisonment in my room, I coughed them up.

I remember being called out in middle school by a teacher accusing me of smoking. I was mortified; not only was I a misfit with a mullet perm (yes, you read that correctly) and extreme acne on my forehead, but I was also now a smoker?!?! Thanks, Mr. Science Teacher, for that added boost of confidence. "No, I do not smoke. My mom does," I cried. I still get upset just thinking about that moment. All I wanted was for my mom not to smoke, and here, my teacher thinks it was me! Even worse, it was a teacher I looked up to and respected. I was devastated that he would even think for a second that I would do something so terrible and disgusting, but I guess that was only because he thought *I* was terrible and disgusting. I was better than that, I had a vision for my life, and smoking was not one of them.

Yet, there I was, smoking a pack every other day. I could blame it on the failed marriage(s), my dad dying, the unexpected deaths of my aunt and ex-mother-in-law, my son being born premature, and my second husband's continued adultery; but NO, I don't blame people, places, or things for my behavior. I must never show weakness.

So instead, I convinced myself that I just loved to smoke. Really? I tried again and again to stop. Five days here, ten days there. I think I even got to 30 days at one point. But, inevitably, I'd pick up another pack blaming it on a stressful day or situation, forgetting that I don't blame people, places, or things for my behavior, right?!? Hmmm, could it be that I might be powerless over smoking? No, that can't be it. I'm a strong-willed woman. Dammit, I can quit!

When I was younger, I could have a few cigarettes while drinking with friends on a Friday night and not smoke again until the following Friday. When I became pregnant with my first son, I quit immediately, no problem! Not to mention I vowed when I was a little girl that I would NEVER smoke.

Yet, attempt after failed attempt, I found myself with another pack in my purse, hair full of smoke, air freshers everywhere to mask the smell, and, dare I say it, a yellowish-stained fingernail. OMG seriously?? Who am I? I would buff that baby daily, even go and get a manicure to mask it, only later to find the shellac nail polish stained and have to buff it out again. I can't believe I am writing this all out in this book, but heck, I am all about transparency, and dang it, you are going to see all of me! Because secrets keep us sick, not safe, and if I can't do it, who am I to suggest you do?

This is starting to get out of control, right? And I *wanted* to believe it was getting out of control. But there I was, with another pack of smokes in my purse, day in and day out, puffing once and buffing twice. It became a way of life. Did I mention I meditate, practice yoga, and am a health and wellness nut? What in the holy heck was I doing? My goals and dreams are massive, and all of them point to health, wellness, and the pursuit of happiness, so why on God's Green Earth would I keep finding myself buying another pack of Marlboros?

Then it hit me!

PAUSE

I need to Pause and get the monkeys back in their cage.

PEEL

I was sitting in meditation one morning when this powerful revelation came over me, and I swear to you, it HIT me right in the middle of the forehead, right where your third eye sits.

REVEAL

I smoke to avoid truly going after my dreams of being an Emotional Fitness Trainer, Empowerment Coach, and Published Author. It was an excuse I didn't even realize I was telling myself so that I didn't have to pursue the goals I had been talking about for more than ten years! I used this excuse subconsciously to give myself permission to *not* sign up for yoga teaching training; to *not* get back on that treadmill; to *not* sign up for the 10K. It was an excuse for why my finances sucked, my closet was cluttered, and my 100th new idea to reinvent myself never stuck.

I smoked therefore, I was a smoker!

You don't know what you don't know until you know you don't know... and now I knew I was hiding behind my yellowish stained fingernail, using that as armor to protect me from taking a risk on myself.

At that moment, the Truth and the Lie were exposed.

Truth: *I am hiding behind the worthiness of my desires and dreams by smoking.*

versus

Lie: *I am a smoker that will never measure up.*

I had two choices:

Eat the Banana or Die. (Probably literally with this example.)

HEAL

The Truth was I was better than that image I had painted for myself. I was trapped in that permed-mullet-haired 12-year-old girl's body, sitting in science class believing I wasn't good enough or worthy enough to be seen. I allowed that limiting belief to protect me from taking a risk on myself. It is much safer to be complacent—no one can reject you, make fun of you, or talk about you behind your back. This is an unsafe belief that no longer serves me today. I was confusing comfort for safety.

It's a FACT!! That is why every time I smoked, I felt like I was in control. Until I wasn't. I loved smoking! Not because it made my hair and breath smell amazing, or because it gave my index finger its beautiful yellowish stain. I loved smoking because it was a part of my unsafe belief system I used to protect myself from the possibility of rejection and failure. The more I smoked, the more I validated and reinforced this erroneous belief and the more evidence I found to support it.

Now fully aware of why I loved to smoke, I had to decide to stop the insanity or continue living a lie. Seeing my inner child, I had to take action and peel back the Banana that was no longer protecting; instead, it was hurting me. Not just physically but mentally and spiritually. Once I realized the *"what"* I was doing, behind the *"why"* I was doing it, I was finally able to let go and grow into the woman I was born to be and that my inner child deserved. I can now say that removing this unsafe belief gave me the courage to stop smoking and the permission and freedom I needed to pursue my dreams.

I chose to Eat the Banana and now am a certified, non-smoking yoga teacher... who doesn't teach yoga.

But my closet looks amazing!

Namaste

11

It's Not About the D

It's not about the D. And by D, I mean divorce; or shall I say divorc*es*. As I scanned my life in the relationship department, while looking for pivotal moments to use the 5-Step Method, relationships in the love category were blaring. Heck, the relationships in *all* areas of my life flashed the distress signal, S.O.S. Jobs, family, friends, and men all took a hit. I would find ways to justify my relationships—I would tell myself I wasn't close to my family because I grew up in a single-family household and wasn't close to my dad or his side of the family; I didn't make a lot of friends because I moved a lot; I didn't like a job because I felt it wasn't the right fit for me; and, perhaps the best one yet, men are jerks and they always cheat. And yes, while most of those justifications may be true, they are NOT the truth as to why I job-hopped, kept myself isolated, and was working on my third divorce before it ever started.

The Truth was deeper than my actions and the actions of the people I chose to surround myself with, or those I chose to avoid altogether. The Truth was rooted in my unsafe beliefs about who I thought I was. My unsafe beliefs made me think I was unlovable, unworthy, and not good enough. I believed I was the black sheep; the loser loner who didn't deserve to have the "Leave it to Beaver" family, the successful career, or a partner who loved me unconditionally.

My Ego looked for situations and people to feed its sickness to reinforce the erroneous beliefs I had about myself. As long as I kept leaving jobs or changing careers, I would feel validated in my truth that I was not smart enough or talented enough to make it to the top. As long as I didn't invest in people, I could continue to feel that I wasn't worth their time. As long as I kept seeking out men I knew were not available (mentally, spiritually, and perhaps physically), I wouldn't have to expose myself and be intimately vulnerable. As long as I continued to play small, I never had far to fall.

This vicious cycle led me down a path of isolation, rejection, and many failed relationships in the love department. I continued to act as if I was better than the people, places, and things that rejected me when I wasn't available to receive or hear the truth in front of me. Instead, I ignored the signs, justified my actions, and repeated the behaviors that inevitably produced the same results.

The Power of the Pause allowed me to slow down just enough to see, hear, and feel what my gut was trying to tell me all along. If we look at science, our brains don't develop the analytical thinking filter until six years of age. That tells me that everything I experienced up to that point went straight past rational thinking and directly into the memory dump. I'd say the bank, but dump feels more appropriate. It was all garbage and most certainly stunk like trash. Any thought, feeling, or emotion that makes you feel less than others is garbage, and it was time to take mine out to the curb.

Applying the 5-Step Method, I "cleaned house," placed my unsafe beliefs in garbage bags, and removed them once and for all. Looking back on my earliest memories of where the unsafe beliefs were created, I placed one after another into the trash—starting with my belief that I wasn't worthy of love. Where did this thought first get planted? How could a precious little girl with her full life ahead of her begin to think for a second that she was unworthy of love?

LOVE is LIFE. LIFE is LOVE.

We are all here to be loved, feel loved, give love, and receive love.

Yet at a very young age I adopted the belief system that I was not. As young, innocent minds incapable of filtering out the Truth from the untruth, we are highly vulnerable and susceptible to Identity Sabotage. We fall victim to our surroundings and the things we are exposed to. What we see, hear, and feel are so real to us that they *must* be true. We begin comparing how we feel to how others show up in our lives. If someone looks happy and we feel sad, that must mean *we* are broken, or something is wrong with *us*. If someone tells us we aren't good at math and we see a fellow classmate excelling at it, that must mean *we* are stupid. If we see happy households with a mom and dad and ours is chaotic with an absent father and overstressed mother, then that must mean *we* are less than deserving of anything different.

We compare, compete, and contrast our perceptions with our reality. We begin to play small and, little by little, shift our mindset to one of lack. We develop coping mechanisms, self-defense strategies, and unsafe beliefs that make us feel safe and protected. Repeated daily, these actions set out to reinforce our negative mindset to the point that it creates a new comfort in a place where we feel discomfort.

Even worse, we grow accustomed to this false sense of relief that anytime things feel good, we see it as if something is wrong and look for ways to create chaos to balance our beliefs. Crazy right?

I realize that this is a lot to download into one chapter, so I am breaking it up into digestible stories to prove this theory correct without causing overload to your nervous system or crashing your hard drive. In this chapter, we will PEEL back the unsafe beliefs around LOVE and feeling unworthy regarding relationships.

STORYTIME

Back to my third divorce. As I mentioned at the beginning of this chapter, I was headed into my third divorce before it even began. You see, up to a point before meeting my now-husband, I was a bum magnet. I honestly believe that if it weren't for him glitching the hardware system in my mind, it would have been another failed attempt at love and marriage. I never laughed so hard after watching *Pretty Woman* later in my adult years than when she explained herself as a "bum magnet." I could totally relate. Now, if any of my exes read this book, I mean that with the most unconditional love and respect, and I honestly mean that. I appreciate everyone's journey and believe in my heart that we are all doing the best we can in life with what we have and what we know.

I have learned that NO ONE can complete YOU despite what Renée Zellweger said in *Jerry Maguire*. When a lost Soul searches for love, they often attract another lost Soul looking for the same. They may be able to complement you and enhance your life, but NO ONE can *complete* you. The only one responsible for your happiness is YOU. The only one that can complete YOU is YOU.

That said, I was looking for love in all the wrong places (unconsciously) to fill my unsafe belief that I was unworthy of love. From my earliest memory, I would attract the bad guy. This guy would be one of two types—one that would make me feel worthy, or one that made me feel needed. If I landed a man that I thought would make me feel worthy, he would be the type that felt unattainable. He was either the jock in school or the highly successful narcissistic businessman with a fancy house and car who traveled the world.

The other type of man was one that I felt I could help. He was the bad boy and the life of the party. He needed love, and I would be the one to change him by giving him all of me. Both scenarios left one crucial part out... ME! I was either trying to prove myself worthy of love or desperate to give it away at the cost of losing myself in the process. This behavior and self-seeking gratification lead to heartache, lower self-esteem, depression, and eventually dependency on alcohol.

When we look outside of ourselves to fill the gaping hole within us, we end up with a bigger hole. Only true love of Self and a Higher Power can fill that void.

One day when I wasn't looking, and without my permission, there was a glitch in the operating system. It was an unforgettable experience. I was minding my own business, focusing on myself, my children, and my career, when two of my closest girlfriends came over to visit. The three of us shared a bottle of wine while catching up on each other's lives. One was online dating and the other was going through a divorce. I was just ending a breakup for the 15th time with the same man—the same man I married, divorced, and started dating again. (Yes, Banana man.)

My girlfriend, who was online dating at the time, shared some stories of the guys she talked to while beaming from ear to ear. She was happy, and we were happy for her. So happy for her, in fact, that my other girlfriend thought it would be cute to scroll for more eligible bachelors for her to go out with. When she said no, my other girlfriend suggested I reactive *my* dating account so we could browse our other friend's account. Two glasses of wine in, this sounded like a brilliant idea. Until she started messaging guys FROM MY ACCOUNT.

When it finally dawned on me that these messages to random guys would come from *my* account and not my girlfriend's, I grabbed the phone and said, "We are done!" Then I thought, *Holy Crap, what if they respond!* Usually, this type of distraction (**Deflect Emotional**

Response) would have been my go-to, but this time, I was working on myself an not looking to date. I knew my old behaviors to fill the void would only lead to further disappointment, self-loathing, and shame. Besides, I would be back with my ex by the following week anyways, so what was the point?

Yes, that was my pattern—one week off, three weeks on. Repeat. Looking back, it makes me want to wrap my arms around my past self and love her up like no other. Actually, I do this often. I have come to love and respect my past self because she went through all of it so I could be the woman I am today.

The following day I awoke to a message from one of the guys we (well, my girlfriend) had reached out to. I was mortified. What was I going to tell him? *Oh, yeah... Hi. About that message... it wasn't actually* from *me, nor was it intended to be* for *me; we were looking at guys for our friend.* That sounds ridiculous, but it is exactly what I said. He surprisingly got a good laugh out of it and proceeded to share his story with me. Reluctantly, I listened and entertained this crazy connection over the dating app for a few weeks before going against my better judgment and giving him my number. I laugh as I type this when I say "better judgment," like anything from my past history would lead you or myself to believe better judgment was one of my attributes.

I digress.

I gave him my number, and we texted each other for a little while before taking the next step of actually talking on the phone. When he called me, my heart sank to the bottom of my stomach, and I swore I would be sick. I couldn't believe I was actually going through with this and talking to him. But that is exactly what I did, and OMG, his voice! He had a voice that spoke to my Soul. I didn't realize it at the time, but I knew something about his voice was different. *He* was different. I wasn't used to "different." I was used to my two types of guys, and he was neither. He glitched the system! Thanks to my girlfriend and the Universe, the rest, as they say, is history. Not only did he break the vicious cycle I was in with my ex, but he also proved all my other theories about men wrong.

My world was shaken! So, of course, I had to do what any woman would do when Mr. Right was standing before her, offering unconditional love. I went into full-blown sabotage mode. I did everything I could to make him run, cheat, and leave me. Nothing worked. NOTHING! I realized years later that sometimes the Universe gives us what we NEED, not what we THINK we need or WANT. And boy, did it deliver.

Over the course of 10 years I learned lessons, uncovered ugly truths, and reprogrammed many unsafe beliefs about myself, all because of a tiny glitch in my operating system. I realized that I was 100% responsible for how I showed up and what I attracted into my life. I learned that I chose to be distant from family just as much as they may have been distant from me. I discovered that other people's actions have more to do with how they see and feel about themselves than it has anything to do with me. I began to understand that I was seeking out pain in advance to avoid being let down or being proven wrong. I literally became the victim of my own misery.

I created it every day and chose to show up for it willingly. The more we become open to the fact that how people behave is simply a reflection of how they see themselves, everything changes. It by no means condones their bad or hurtful behavior, but it sure does take the pressure off us when thinking WE are to blame for their actions. This goes for you, TOO! When we see how our actions are a direct reflection of how we see ourselves, we can begin to give ourselves some grace, love, and compassion. We permit ourselves to start healing. Never shame, blame, or guilt yourself for actions in the past. You were doing the best you could with what you had and what you knew back then. It's not your fault you fell victim to Identity Sabotage by the Ego.

During a deep meditation, I was contemplating this realization. At the root cause of the condition, it is not our fault we fall victim to the Ego. These mind viruses feed our Ego without us knowing it or without our permission. We are victims of the Ego. True Identity Sabotage at its finest! I call it the DARK SIDE of the Force. Just like in *Star Wars*.

There is a "Dark Side" on this planet—a "negative energy" that's only purpose is to seek out the Light and destroy it. It does this by hijacking our "inner compass" and resetting it to HATE of Self.

> *The chains that keep you bound to the past are not the actions of another person. They are your own anger, stubbornness, lack of compassion, jealousy, and blaming others for your choices. It is not other people that keep you trapped; it is the entitled role of victim that you enjoy wearing. There is a familiarness to pain that you enjoy because you get a payoff from it. When you figure out what that payoff is, then you will finally be on the road to freedom.*

~ *Shannon Alder*

When I first read that quote, I wanted to puke. It made me angry. It made me feel an emotion that I didn't like, and that emotion was humility. After sitting with this for many hours in contemplation during meditation, I was able to say humbly, *Yes*, I *have* been playing the victim to my past and allowing it to show up in the present. I knew I had to make a change if I was going to start seeing and feeling differently. The reason my relationship works today is that I did something different. Even though it wasn't my intention, it was enough to create a slight shift that led to an even bigger one.

This is where science and spiritually come together. To create new experiences to erase the emotions linked to the old ones, we must override our unsafe beliefs.

But how do we create NEW experiences when our unconscious mind runs the show? The simple act of acknowledging this is happening to us and accepting that we have become addicted to this way of thinking awakens our "inner intelligence." It activates a slight shift within our physiology and psychology of the mind-body connection.

The Truth and the Lie were exposed.

Truth: *I was a willing participant in the misery I perceived.*

versus

Lie: *I am unlovable and unworthy of unconditional love.*

I had two choices:

Eat the Banana or Die.

Eating the Banana meant taking full responsibility for the part I chose to play. It meant I had to accept the Truth no matter how ugly it was to see. This is why most people continue living the lie.

When the Truth is too painful to digest, we would rather starve than eat it. But when the hunger pang becomes too intense, we find ourselves at the jumping-off point.

We can go on to the bitter end or accept the fact that we were merely surviving. I was hungry.

I ate the Banana!

12

It's Not About the Lobster

When engaging with other humans, we will undoubtedly from time to time find ourselves on the receiving end of their emotional discharge. Our Emotional Fitness plays a role in how we engage or disengage. Both options have possible side effects ranging from catastrophic failure to harmonious well-being. Yes, the swing is that dramatic, depending on how you choose to respond.

Coexisting is part of life. Unless we choose to live thousands of miles away, up in the lost mountains of you-can't-see-me, we will encounter people. From casual to extremely intimate, we will come in close contact with other people's trauma. Just like us, they have unsafe beliefs and emotional baggage left unchecked. Despite how cute it sounds to help them unpack, it is not our place to do so. Our only job is to not create more luggage.

We do this by checking our own.

When someone upsets us, moves us off our baseline, or causes emotional discord within us, there are a few essential questions to ask yourself.

What unsafe beliefs about the person's actions are affecting me?

Is it possible they feel the same way?

How can I use this experience to heal, not harm?

When we look for similarities instead of differences, our hearts open, allowing us to respond with compassion. Opening our eyes to see the person instead of the action, we shift our perspective, creating a meaningful connection between us.

Unfortunately, this is not how many of us interact. Instead, we focus on the differences, take things personally, and close our hearts and minds to others. We project, protect, deflect, and redirect instead of connect. We separate and defend our point of view, express how we are right and they are wrong for feeling the way they do, and shut down all communication. We give them the silent treatment, become passive-aggressive, and even lash out to hurt.

When we listen to understand, we open a new line for communication, perception, and connection. Treating others the way we wish to be treated and understood, we see them through our eyes, ears, and hearts. Love is the easier, softer way.

The Ego blocks, separates, and destroys human connection by telling us we are different, better than, or unworthy. We compete, compare, and contrast with each other, delusionally thinking we are under attack. Because of the Ego, we feel alone, lost, and unseen.

We cannot grow if we do not evolve our reptilian brain's way of coping. Emotional Fitness is our best line of defense. We change when we awaken and strengthen the oldest part of our brain. Pausing before every new reaction, asking the questions to qualify the best emotional response, we create new pathways leading us closer to the Truth.

This simple exercise can transform our relationships with ourselves and others. And as we know, we are wired for connection, not disconnection. Yet those wires have been crossed, disconnected, and frayed somewhere along the way. Luckily, it is not permanent and can be repaired and restored to use as intended.

STORYTIME

One day (well, not just *any* day; it was Father's Day), my husband and I went for a drive. As I mentioned in the chapter "It's Not About the Banana," recalling the exact events that took place was hard, but remembering how they made me feel stayed with me. For whatever reason, his daughter was not with us that day. And being a stepdad to my two children meant they were with their father. I remember all three of them acknowledging him, and my daughter even brought him his favorite coffee drink, an iced brava mocha with whip cream.

As we continued on our little country drive, I remember asking him how he was feeling, assuming he must be upset that he was not spending the day with his daughter. He replied that he was fine (red flag) and was enjoying the time with me while looking forward to some steak and lobster once we returned home.

We went to the fancy market to pick up the best cut of beef and pick out the unlucky lobster to pair it with. Upon returning home, he asked me to prepare the lobster while he fired up the grill. Sensing he was lying to me about being fine, I reluctantly held back what I wanted to say. Instead, I smiled and said, "Absolutely." My intention was never for him to make any of his Father's Day dinner, but he was the grill master, and I sure didn't want to overcook the meat.

As we walked into the kitchen, I ignored his energy and what my gut told me. I could see he was off and slightly irritated. He was short, off-putting, and annoyed at the smallest of things. I went straight into my emotional response, **Protect**, and started to search the internet for the best way to cook the lobster.

While I was reading directions on how to boil versus bake, he cracked. All the feelings he had been stuffing escaped, and I was now the lucky recipient of his emotional discharge. "Never mind, I'll just do it myself," he snapped.

The perfect opportunity to PAUSE was presented, and instead, I hit fast forward. All the shots were being fired, and I took each as a personal hit. Not looking at the event for what it was, I fired back.

With both of our unsafe beliefs engaged, we fought. **Project** and **Redirect** were our tools, and we used them like we were in the fight of our lives. With our window of tolerance closing, we began to throw sticks and stones.

My husband's ammunition:

- *You're doing this on purpose, so I'll have to do everything like I always do!*
- *Why are you so difficult?*
- *You don't even care.*

My ammunition:

- *You're being an ass!*
- *Why are you so stubborn?*
- *You always think you are right.*

Back and forth, we fought for our stance on top of Mount Ego. Not seeing the Banana in the room (or, in this case, the lobster), we disconnected and retreated to our separate corners. Mine was the bedroom where I aggressively folded the laundry, and his was the kitchen and grill. That poor lobster didn't see it coming.

The stories I began to tell myself led me to plan my escape. Redirecting my emotions to avoid dealing with them, I started to develop an exit plan. With all my unsafe beliefs blaring, I blocked them with lies. Lies I believed were my truth. Words like NEVER, ALWAYS, and SHOULD, filled my defense.

Blinded by the Lies, the empathy I felt for my husband not spending Father's Day with his daughter was an absent memory replaced with SELF. Instead of seeing my husband's actions as a cry for love and connection, I ran and took it personally.

It wasn't about the lobster. And it wasn't about me. It was about my husband. My own unsafe beliefs kept me from seeing the Truth. I was that little six-year-old girl coloring outside the lines, being told I didn't care enough. But I did care!... Didn't I? Of course I did, or else I wouldn't be so upset over the stupid lobster. Or was I upset over not feeling good enough to know how to cook it? Maybe I was upset over being told I didn't care when all I do is care. Why can't anyone see how much I care? Could it possibly be because I don't?

The Truth and the Lie were exposed.

Truth: *I do care. But I care too much about what others think than my actual caring for others.*

versus

Lie: *If others criticize me, I must have done something wrong, and no one appreciates me.*

I had two choices:

Eat the Banana or Die.

Emotional Fitness isn't about abandoning our emotional responses; it's about acknowledging when they are happening and decerning when and where to use them appropriately. Being productive, not destructive, we see our part. We own our part.

The Truth was that I lived a lie built on unsafe beliefs that told me I didn't matter. I became so determined to prove to the world that I *did matter* that I failed to see how my actions left others feeling as if *they didn't*.

My husband's feelings were justified based on my actions, not Truth. My feelings were justified based on his actions, not Truth. Truth being, we both cared, but our actions were caring for the wrong reasons.

My husband's unsafe belief was that he must be the provider and do everything to carry out his role of what he thinks a man is. All while doing it with resentment that he is the only one doing anything. In continuing to play this role, he looks for more evidence to reinforce even more resentment until the day comes when he asks his wife to prepare the lobster.

Looking at the event through my husband's eyes, he already "knew" how it was going to play out. He knew he wanted it broiled, not baked. He knew what dish it should be prepared in and what seasoning complemented it best.

Once he saw that I was not on the same page, he immediately took over. Like he always has to do. His unsafe beliefs were once again reinforced.

My unsafe beliefs that if someone is upset, it must be because of something I did and that conflict equals divorce led me to defend and protect, and I knew I had to try something different.

Taking what my husband said to heart, I had to reflect on how my past actions led him to conclude that he had to do everything and that I didn't care. I had to find my part and acknowledge the role I was playing.

Facts are based on evidence, and it was time that I faced them.

I chose to eat the Banana.

Seeing all my husband had been through throughout his life, I began to see how I was adding to his emotional baggage. And I could also see how I was adding more to mine by continuing to bring the past into the present. We were both overloaded.

As I mentioned at the beginning of this chapter, it is not our job to help the other unpack; it is our job to not add more to their baggage by checking our own. The fact was my husband did everything just as he always had. And I added more weight instead of lightening his load, which consequently reinforced his unsafe beliefs. I brought all my drama, trauma, and erroneous beliefs into the relationship without acknowledging or accepting any of his.

I took advantage of his strength and willingness to provide, support, and protect. I didn't believe it was real or would last, so I took what I could for as long as possible. I was so used to being the victim and surviving that, at first, it felt good to relax and do nothing. I even convinced myself that I deserved it after everything I had been through. The problem was that I took more than I gave, and it was time to give back.

Another Truth and Lie appeared.

Truth: *I am deserving of unconditional love, just because, not because.*

versus

Lie: *Everyone leaves; nothing good lasts long.*

I had two more choices:

Eat the Banana or Die.

The evidence of my past relationships led me to believe that all relationships end, so why bother? My actions made my husband feel like I didn't care, and my unsafe beliefs reinforced them.

Nothing in life lasts forever. Relationships come and go. Seasons change. People change. This is a fact supported by evidence. So why not take the good with the bad? And who's to say what is or isn't? To experience joy, we must know sadness. To appreciate success, we must first fail. To see the light, we must understand the darkness. To rise, we must fall. To help others heal, we must know the hurt.

After an hour of raging on the pages of my "shitty first draft" journal (thank you, Anne Lamott, for this therapeutic practice), I could see my part and start cleaning up my side of the street, starting with the lobster.

My husband was right. I knew how much he did for us and how spending time with family meant so much to him. Knowing how the day was going to play out, I could have taken the time to better prepare ahead of time. Instead, I got so caught up in my own drama that I had little time to worry about the events ahead. The Truth was I was premediating events to reinforce my unsafe beliefs, then tried to use them in my defense to prove my case.

The Truth can be a big pill to swallow that gets caught in your throat going down. This is why it can seem easier to continue living the Lie. I could continue playing out the same old story or end it right here, right now. I was done living a run-on sentence that left me exhausted with no victory lap to celebrate. It was time to wave the white checkered flag.

I ate another Banana. (Too bad metaphorical Bananas don't have potassium)

I left the bedroom with much of the laundry still unfolded and looked at my husband with empathy and compassion. I apologized for making him feel the way he did, regardless of my intentions. It was in my actions that he felt unseen. The emotional discharge experienced that day had nothing to do with the lobster. It was the events leading up to it that did.

The day ended with my husband and I enjoying dinner together, sharing vulnerable stories of our past that connected us to that present, harmonious moment.

It was never about the lobster.... But he was good!

13

It's Not About the Relapse

I know I said writing the Banana Chapter was the hardest but writing this chapter was the hardest of all for different reasons. But I knew if I didn't write it and tell the whole truth in complete transparency, I would not only be doing you a disservice, but I would also be dishonoring the lesson I had to learn in order to write it.

Three years into my recovery from alcohol, I was feeling good. I began rebuilding trust within my family, friends, community, and work. I was sponsoring women, chairing meetings, and stepping out of the box I had previously committed to staying in. I was trusting myself enough to revisit areas of my life I had given up exploring. Maybe, just maybe, I was ready? Perhaps, just maybe, I could dare to try again? I mean, I was sober for three years. I quit smoking, I ate healthily, I gave up meat, and meditated daily. I could handle it!

What I failed to realize is that "looking the part" does not "make the part," and the gap in between was where my addiction and unsafe beliefs lurked, just waiting for me to fall in and take me down once and for all. This is where the Universe gives us what we need and not always what we want or *think* we need. It is all-knowing, all-loving, and all-supporting. Even when it feels like it is out to get us, it really is out to guide, nurture, and grow us. The more we heal, the more that will be revealed, which is precisely what happened.

As I continued to work on this book, I became a yoga teacher and meditation guide, and I graduated from IIN to be a health coach specializing in gut health. I enrolled in school to earn my BA as an Ayurveda practitioner and was promoted to a high-level corporate position within my company. **(Deflect and Redirect Emotional Response.)** What could possibly go wrong? Nothing, I thought! I was living my dreams, finally owning my space, and speaking my truth. I had arrived! However, in the deepest corners of my mind lurked shadows so dark I never dared to look. Why in the world would I revisit places in my mind that would hurt me, destroy my spirit, make me feel weak, and expose my ugliest of secrets? I would NEVER! I was told that secrets keep us sick, but I didn't buy that. Secrets kept me SAFE, and that is where I planned to stay. Safe in my bubble, I continued with my plans, my way.

As long as I was meditating, eating right, not drinking, and being better than I was yesterday, I had all the right ingredients to make my dreams a reality. I had never felt more alive. I started creating content to share with anyone who would listen. I blindly opened up my business without thinking twice. I had giant visions and didn't apologize for daring to dream, no matter the cost. Little by little, my passion became an obsession and a new addiction to feed. In the 12-Step Program we are told that we are destined to lose anything we put before our recovery. Another suggestion I chose to ignore; besides I was too busy for meetings, I was going places. I was obviously recovered in the drinking department. I mean, look at me—every day people told me how amazing I was doing, how I brought light to every room I walked in, how I made people feel better about themselves just by spending time with them. Every day I pushed myself to do more. I signed up for an intensive four-day motivational seminar that inspired me to go all in. I was so invested in *proving myself* that I became blinded to the fact I was actually *losing myself* in the process.

The day finally came when the cost I was paying was too high. My spiritual bank was overdrawn, with no savings to fall back on. Just because I looked "the part," played "the part," and acted "the part" did not mean I was ready to BE "the part." Those secrets I chose to keep hidden—the dark shadows that lurked in the deepest corners of my mind—were still there. No matter how many things I put in front of me to distract me, they were still there. That gap between acting the part and being the part was still there, just waiting for me to slip and fall in.

When you build a foundation on unstable ground, the foundation cracks. In those cracks I tripped and landed flat on my face. I don't recall exactly when my mind shifted away from my recovery, nor do I remember when I first thought I was healed, but I know that one day I woke up and decided that a drink sounded like a good idea.

A drink sounded so good, in fact, that I planned out just how and when it would happen. Despite all my history of the past and all the promising opportunities for my future, I was "all in" to play in the present.

STORYTIME

It was July 4th, and my husband was going to his friend's house for a BBQ and I was headed to visit my friend two hours north. As I got ready for the day, I was thinking about where to stop to get the alcohol, as it had to be far enough away to avoid bumping into someone I knew. What kind of alcohol was I going to drink? Do I go back to my wine box? No, I don't want to return to that dark place; I'll do the mini wine bottles instead. All these plans raced through my head while talking to my husband about what he was bringing to the BBQ and how I would meet up with him later. Everything sounded perfect! I had convinced myself that I wasn't actually an alcoholic; when I drank "alcoholically," it was due to my past life events. **(Projection Emotional Response Blaring.)** I mean, seriously, who wouldn't drink after being cheated on, divorced twice, taken to court for outlandish claims on my character, having people you thought were family turn their back on you, almost losing your first child due to complications during childbirth, losing your father shortly after you were finally establishing a healthy relationship, being made fun of in school, and lied to your entire life? I'm not the person I was back then, I told myself repeatedly. I have a life I love, a family I adore, and a promising future. I would never go back to that place. I was drinking "alcoholically" due to the situations in my life at the time.

On my two-hour drive north I became more convinced I was doing the right thing. I deserved a day to play and be silly. I was working so hard and doing so well that I owed it to myself to take a break. Why not? Everyone else had been slacking off while I was busy chasing my dreams and sacrificing myself in the process. Besides, it was just for today! So that is what I did; I walked into that store with one mission—buy two small airplane bottles of wine and enjoy (ok, I guess that's *two* missions).

Mission accomplished!

For the next 30 minutes I stared at those little bottles of relief and had a moment of PAUSE, trying to replay the tape in my mind about why this was or wasn't a good plan. The more I tried to remember why I had stopped drinking, the more I forgot. I opened that first bottle and took a swig. Then another. Then another until it was gone. The feeling of relief that ran down my throat and warmed my belly felt like a long-lost friend I hadn't seen in years. I was back home. I felt comfort where I had been feeling discomfort. I felt calm where I had been feeling anxiety. I felt peace where I heard noise. Everything in that moment felt right, safe, and familiar—no judgment, no expectations, no proving myself.

Just me and my best friend Chardonnay. We were reunited, and it felt so good.

Those dark, lurking shadows were gone, as were the secrets I kept locked away. I was free from the misery I didn't even realize I was chained to. I was free from the past I was trying so hard to rewrite. I was free from the future I still didn't believe I deserved. With every drink I took, I felt more removed from it all, which explains why I kept drinking that day.

My visit with my friend was beautiful, and we had a great time catching up and listening to music from her era while laughing, singing, and dancing around the house. I still don't think she knew I had been drinking that day, as I hadn't overshot my mark. It wasn't until my drive back home to meet my husband at our friend's house, where they were having a beautiful BBQ with a full bar, that my mark rocketed into the twilight zone. I immediately "told on myself" that I had been drinking, which my husband didn't believe at first, but it only took a few more seconds for him to realize that I was telling the truth. From there, I was off to the races, drinking, laughing, chatting it up with strangers as if I had known them my entire life, and making lavish business plans for the future.

As the night ended, my husband and I went to bed without talking much more about it. When I woke the next morning, the familiar feelings I used to dread set in. Remorse. Shame. Guilt. What in the hell did I do? How could I have allowed this to happen? Did I throw away three years of sobriety for this? Then *embarrassment* came knocking; flashbacks of conversations and behaviors from the night before reminded me quickly why I quit drinking. Oh hello, loneliness and despair. I remember you. How quickly we forget the bad times! I immediately went into damage control mode and tried my best to clean up the destruction (albeit brief, but destruction nonetheless) that I had caused over the past 24 hours. **(Redirect and Project.)**

I came clean to my children, apologized to my husband and our friends, and just like that, was forgiven.

"Oh, how dark it is before the dawn."

I didn't have a single drink for the next two weeks. I did everything possible to return to the happy place I was before my relapse. But no amount of meditation, yoga, or juicing could bring that version of me back. It was dark. I was dark. Lights OUT! My hope, will, and passions were gone. I could not find the motivation or inspiration to write, connect, or do any of the things I had been doing in sobriety. At the time I was still working toward earning my BA, but eventually had to drop a class because it was too much for me to handle. For the life of me, I couldn't understand *why* I was feeling the way I was.

This disconnect from my Soul-Self ultimately led me to another drink. And for two and a half months, that's what I did—drink, lie, and hide what I was doing.

Eventually, it caught up to me. You can only run for so long before you find yourself waving the white flag or living under a bridge. I chose to wave that flag! I have no doubt what happened next was a gift from God and proof that the Universe actually does have our back 100%.

In one of my drunken moments, I called a treatment center looking for relief. The obsession to drink was back, and its claws were in deep. I couldn't stop, and believe me, I wanted to stop. I wanted nothing more than to go back in time before that day when I thought I could have *just one* drink. I was right back where I had left off three years ago, only worse. The cravings came out of nowhere and the only light I could see at the end of this tunnel was most definitely a freight train headed straight for me.

I cried to the lady on the phone and explained my situation. As she listened and asked me more questions, I began to panic. The thoughts of going back into treatment flooded me with fear, worry, and doubt. How could I possibly do this again? I quickly hung up and began to pretend that I could pull through. That night, as my husband looked at me with a helpless and hopeless gaze, I did everything I could to convince him I would be okay.

"I'm headed to a yoga retreat with my sponsor in the morning," I said. "That will fix me and bring me back to the person I once was. I know it will." He didn't have much to say. How could he?

When I awoke the following day, he had already left for work along with my car keys. He took them to work, hoping it would prevent me from going to the store to buy more alcohol. It didn't. As I began to pack my three-night bag of yoga gear, I couldn't take it any longer. I *had* to go to the store. I had to pack *something* to get me through. So I walked two miles in the dark, pouring rain to the store to buy my supply and calm the voices in my head. The moment I walked out of the store, I began drinking the noise away. By the time I reached my house, I was feeling no shame in my pain and finished packing (making sure to stash some bottles away for safekeeping in my bag) before my ride arrived.

My sponsor came to pick me up, and we were off to Costco to pick up supplies for the retreat ahead. The entire time I talked and acted as if I was okay, convinced she didn't notice I was already drunk. As she pumped gas to head out on our three-hour drive, a voice spoke to me. I hadn't heard her in more than two months while I was drinking, but there she was, telling me to call the treatment center again. Without thinking, I did just that. The voice on the other line told me I could admit myself right then and there, so I did. I mustered up all the courage and strength I had left to call my husband and let him know that I would not be gone for three days... I would be gone for 28 instead.

PAUSE

I was scared walking into the facility, yet I was also at peace. Something ignited inside me that had been missing. It wasn't much, but it was something. It took a few days, but as I continued to find humility in my actions, thinking, and behavior, that light burned brighter. Slowly the claws released, and the light was back. I found the willingness to go to those dark corners where the shadows lurked and shine my light on them. I became willing to face my shadows, share my secrets, and allow others to see me. All of me.

One night in treatment leading up to this transformational process, I prayed. I got down on my knees and prayed. I prayed for hope. I prayed for real relief. I prayed for a sign that I was doing the right thing. At that moment, my eye caught a label on my curling iron. Yes, my curling iron—remember, I was packing for a yoga retreat with a bunch of women, so my clothing options and supplies were not the norm for a rehab facility. Talk about being vulnerable. Everyone there had clothes for 28 days, and I had three pairs of yoga pants, one flip-to-my-flops, and a curling iron—another negative side effect of packing while drunk. I don't recommend it. Luckily I wasn't too far from home, and my family brought reinforcements.

PEEL

Back to the curling iron... as I was saying, I was praying for a sign that I had made the right choice by going back to treatment when the label caught my eye. It had my name and the exact date and time I was admitted. It read 11:11 a.m. For those who don't know, 11:11 is a special number and one that I hold very near and dear to my heart. So much so that my friends and family call it out whenever they see it. To me, it's a sign that the Universe is with me, that I am supported and protected. When I saw that time stamp on my admittance label, I broke down and cried. I cried the happiest and most therapeutic tears of my life. This was a different cry than the cry in that mental hospital shower; this was a cry of true surrender and relief. The relief I had been praying for was here.

REVEAL

I realized I wasn't broken; I was just disconnected from my power source. I had been focusing all my attention and energy on the future, or on running away from my past, that the cord that connects me to my source couldn't reach me. I couldn't change the past with my future, no matter how hard I tried. It's by living in the present moment that we find our power. It's in the present that we find peace. From that moment on, my mantra was "I realign with peace in mind" to remind me to stay where my feet are. The only business I have in the past is in healing my inner child, and the only part I have to play in the future is in my actions in the present moment.

For the next 28 days, I did nothing but listen. I was honest about my defense mechanisms, the biggest ones being **deflect** and **redirect**, and the other being overcompensation. Coughing up my defense mechanisms was hard as I had grown accustomed to manipulation to get what I needed or avoid being called out. I knew that if I were going to get to the ROOT cause of WHY I decided to drink and ignore what it was that I was hiding from, I would have to feel all the feelings and face my shadow self.

When asked if I would lead the yoga and meditation classes at the rehab facility, I declined, despite my natural instinct to say yes. I knew it would be a great distraction and a way to get people to like me, but I wasn't there to make friends with anyone but ME. The crazy part was that even though all I did was show up as my *real* and *authentic* disconnected self, people actually *did* like me. I didn't have to try to fit in, overdo it or pretend to be someone I wasn't. They just liked me as me. This was a new experience.

HEAL

Setting my intentions in the moment and paying attention to my actions throughout the day keeps me in alignment. When the two don't connect, I realign my thinking. When my motives to revisit the past are to reinforce pain or unsafe beliefs, I PAUSE. When my energy is draining because I am tripping out about tomorrow, I PAUSE. I ask myself WHAT am I feeling and I breathe. Right here, right now, I am okay!

When I am living in pain, I am living in the past; when I am living in fear, I am living in the future. It's in the present we find peace. It's in the present we find solutions. It's in the present we LIVE. As I continued to perform daily spot checks and fill in the gaps and cracks with true humility, willingness, and love, I could repair my foundation with TRUTH. My unsafe beliefs that I wasn't worthy of love, success, or becoming a *New York Times* best-selling author led me to drink that day.

The rejections I received from literary agents only reinforced my unsafe belief of not being good enough. The idea that I had to be perfect to be loved prevented me from sharing my secrets and connecting with others. The need to prove myself to the world to feel valued and important only reinforced my belief that I was not enough. It wasn't until I was able to PAUSE in these moments and ask myself WHAT was I feeling that I was able to be real, raw, and honest with myself and with another person.

Getting to the ROOT cause of my conditions that were causing the symptoms that led me to drink, I could remove the mind virus and replace it with one that helps me, not hurts me. Secrets keep us sick because they continue to make us feel different, guilty, shameful, dirty, and less than others. They cut you off from connecting with others and prevent you from experiencing the true unconditional love of self and others.

If you don't believe me, ask yourself this question: do you feel connected to me more now than before? Am I more relatable, likable, and reachable? Do you feel seen, loved, and accepted after hearing my deepest, darkest truth? Does hearing my story give you the courage to connect and do the same? If you answered yes to any of these questions, there is your proof.

The Truth and The Lie were exposed.

Truth: *I don't have to feel ashamed of my pain and suffering.*

versus

Lie: *I must never show weakness and admit my faults.*

I had two choices:

Eat the Banana or Die.

It wasn't about the relapse. It was about learning the lessons I had been avoiding along the way. It was about forgiving myself for my past and not shaming her by ignoring her in the present. It was about being honest with myself to connect to my Truth and others. It was about healing all of me, not just the parts I deemed worthy of seeing. It was part of my story that only I could live to share with you.

In that relapse, I finally let go of the things I could not control, found the courage to change the things I could, and found the willingness to know it was me.

I chose to eat the Banana, one messy bite at a time.

14

It's Not About the Tablecloth

One of the many things I loved about writing this book was taking significant events from my life to apply the 5-Step Method to uncover the lies I had been living as my truth. In sharing my stories over the years, I have come to find that many of you have similar experiences. The beauty in sharing is discovering that we are not alone. Hearing others struggle with similar challenges makes us feel connected and understood. It's not that we find pleasure in hearing that someone else went through what we did; it's more about knowing that someone else understands us.

Feeling seen is a huge part of our basic human needs. Yes, we need food, air, water, and shelter to survive; but to Thrive, we need more. The nature of life is to grow. We water a plant and give it sunlight to grow. Water a human and provide them with sunlight, and you'll get someone with a nice tan who has to pee. We are complex creatures that require a few more ingredients to help us evolve into the spiritual beings we were created to become.

Unfortunately, nowadays, feeling seen has been replaced with "being seen" while trying to keep up with the Kardashians and other materialistic, unrealistic expectations. We think we must look, act, and behave a certain way to feel seen and deemed worthy; but we still don't feel seen when we are noticed because what others see is not who we are.

To feel seen, we must become vulnerable and shed the façade. I don't care how many people say that "money buys happiness, and those who think it doesn't do so because they don't have it." That's a LIE! Money does not buy happiness. Stuff does not bring happiness. And no matter how beautiful your tablecloth is, it won't make you happy. Nor will trying to impress someone over your elegant new linen. (More on this in Storytime.)

To *feel* seen is to share our Truth. To *be* seen is to deny it. To *feel* seen is to feel understood. Understanding nurtures compassion, which develops love and belonging. When we lead with love, we build esteem for Self. Esteem for Self permits us to speak our Truth. When we speak our Truth, we transform our lives.

The need to impress is a cry for help. It's a sign of unworthiness disguised as confidence. Insecurities take the form of overcompensation and manipulation. We hide behind many masks, hoping they will attract the acceptance we desperately seek.

We find ourselves in empty relationships and unfulfilling careers with an underwhelming sense of belonging. Disconnected from our Truth, we feel lost, and life seems meaningless without direction or purpose. We buy shiny new masks, repeating this vicious cycle to avoid looking at ourselves.

When we understand why we do what we do and take an honest look at our actions, reactions, and distractions, we will uncover the Lies we continue to live as our truth. We will begin to let go of things that don't serve us to allow room for things that do.

The ability to laugh at yourself in the process is vital. We can't take ourselves too seriously. We are human. I'm pretty sure human stands for:

Humbly

Understand

Man

And

Nurture

Humility is the key to humor! When we are humble, we learn to let go of the Ego and laugh.

Pride is the throne for Ego to sit. Humility is the gateway for humanity to live.

The more we open our hearts, share our secrets, and become honest with ourselves and others, the more others will do the same.

Laughter is the best medicine to heal. Laughing in the face of the shame our false identity has created, we take away the power it holds over us. Everyone experiences guilt, shame, pain, disappointment, failure, and a deficiency of self-worth.

Everyone!

Even Oprah.

So why do we feel a need to pretend we don't? It's not only hurting you; it's hurting everyone around you. The more we hide, the more we divide.

STORYTIME

It was the month before Thanksgiving, and this was the year we decided to host it at our home. Our first Thanksgiving sitting at the grown-up table I, myself, had set. The time had come to begin new traditions, and I was ready and eagerly willing.

Growing up, we always had Thanksgiving at my grandparent's house. I loved nothing more than going there early to watch my family prepare the bird and make all the sides to go with it. I even had the honor of wearing the "Official Turkey Taster" badge and took my role seriously.

The smells that filled the room and the laughter surrounding it made me feel safe, loved, and seen. Then, of course, there was the table we would all gather around. Beautiful antique China and silverware were strategically placed on the freshly ironed tablecloth accented with the perfect centerpiece. This was my happy place and favorite time of year.

As the years went on, people who surrounded that table came and went. Some never to return as they passed on. But year after year, I wore that badge, set the table, and was marinated in the love it represented.

I had big shoes to fill this Thanksgiving with memories and traditions I couldn't wait to carry on. My shopping list was complete with all the ingredients to create the perfect setting. I even had my father-in-law help my husband peel the potatoes to make Lefse, another one of our family traditions I felt so proud to share with my new in-laws and step-daughter (my bonus child).

My husband came home from visiting his parents one day while I was busy preparing the order in which I would start cooking, baking, and decorating. This would be their first Thanksgiving at our house, and his mom was concerned we didn't have a nice tablecloth for the occasion.

I was mortified, insulted, and humiliated at the thought that I wouldn't have an acceptable tablecloth to showcase our feast. Does she not think I am classy enough? Does she think I am less than? Does she think I am incapable of pulling off a big event like Thanksgiving?

Of course I had a fancy tablecloth! Well, I might not actually have it yet, but I will! Not only would my tablecloth be fancy, but my presentation will be to die for.

My obsession with impressing took over, and I was all consumed with creating the most spectacular table setting she had ever seen. The Project, Protect, Deflect, and Redirect emotional responses all came to join the S*!t Show.

After countless hours spent scrolling Amazon and days of shopping at all the stores that might carry a tablecloth worthy of the occasion, I finally found her. She was perfect! All the colors of fall were represented while still maintaining a sophisticated elegance.

When it arrived, I quickly ironed it out and placed it on our table. Admiring its beauty and how it perfectly set the stage, I felt as if something was missing. I know—it needed placemats. Back to the store I went to find the perfect placemats to accent the tablecloth... oh and glassware— we needed better glassware. And cloth napkins.

Now back home, I added my new treasures to the table. And that's when it hit me—you can't have cloth napkins without cute rings to place them in. What about the centerpiece? Back to the store I went, in search of all the items I would need to create the most breathtaking centerpiece and table setting anyone had ever seen.

Later that night, three days before the big show, the table was set. Yet something was still missing. I know! It needed a runner to give it more personality. Off to the store yet again to find the perfect runner to pair with that gorgeous tablecloth. I purchased three, just to be sure, as well as a centerpiece placemat to showcase the centerpiece.

Finally it was complete. I took pictures to show my friends and talked about how beautiful it was. I was so proud of myself and the gorgeous table setting.

Uh-oh, Thanksgiving is tomorrow, and I haven't even begun baking the pies, making the Lefse, or prepping the stuffing. With the table ready for its grand reveal, I went straight to the kitchen and got to work. I even went as far as buying a new apron to really look the part. No shame in my game, ladies!

I'm not sure what time it was before my head hit the pillow that night, but I'm almost certain I didn't sleep a wink before it was time to get up and start the bird. As my husband put the oversized turkey that could feed 20 (we were feeding eight) in the oven, I exhaled. The house *must* smell like Thanksgiving before everyone arrives.

I did it! I made Thanksgiving all by myself. (Yes, my husband helped too.) Everything was perfect. Except me. I was covered in sweat, flour, and glitter (the glitter was from the centerpiece I had spent hours putting together the night before).

I laid out my clothes, hopped in the shower, and got ready for show-time. My hair was curled, my face was on, and my outfit was on point. I looked "the part" and was ready to shine.

As the kids arrived, I was eager to show them the beautiful table setting and point out who was to sit where. The candles were lit, the music was playing, and the Lefse was on display, each piece perfectly placed on its special platter.

The turkey was ready and sitting on the kitchen counter as we began to find our seats. My in-laws were the only two people yet to arrive, and I didn't want anyone to mess up the table before she could see it. I asked everyone not to touch anything as we waited for them to arrive. God bless my family for entertaining the crazy that was on full display that day.

With minutes to spare, I hear my in-laws pull up.

"They're here," I shouted, beaming from ear to ear with anticipation and excitement. I couldn't wait for her to see the presentation I had awaiting her.

I quickly went to the door to let them both in, only to find my father-in-law holding the salad in his hands. But no mother-in-law. I'm sure she's driving separately, I told myself, as she would do this from time to time. As my husband took the salad bowl to its appropriate place on the table, my father-in-law told us that she wouldn't be coming. She wasn't feeling well.

The silence in the room was deafening as everyone's jaws dropped to the floor, staring at me with a look of disappointment. Disappointment that she wouldn't be there, of course, but more so that all my effort was now for nothing. It was obvious that I made such a big deal over my mother-in-law being impressed with the table that my family felt as if they were the sideshow.

I couldn't believe what my ears were trying to tell me and what my brain was trying to process. She's not coming?! All this work, all this time and energy spent on making this Thanksgiving perfect and a table setting worthy of a Queen, and she's not coming? Thank goodness I took pictures! At least then I can show her what she missed.

As we started to pass the side dishes around the table and enjoy a delicious meal, we laughed, shared stories, and made memories together. Despite my obsessions, a new family tradition was born and has since delivered many more dysfunctional Thanksgivings to remember.

Cleaning up that night, I was reminded of something my daughter had shared with me. Earlier that week, as I was frantically trying to make Thanksgiving perfect, she said, "Mom, it doesn't matter how the table looks; all that matters is who surrounds it."

The Truth and the Lie were served with a setting made for one.

Truth: *I am enough and have everything I need.*

versus

Lie: *In order to be accepted and loved, I must look "the part."*

I had two choices:

Eat the Banana or Die.

Peeling back the Banana while reflecting on the event, it was easy to see where I should have paused—the moment my baseline went off its rails. Up until the point my husband mentioned the tablecloth, I was good. I understood the true meaning of Thanksgiving and was grateful for the beautiful family I was about to share it with.

After it was mentioned, my baseline took a hard right, jumped on the insane train, and rode it all the way to crazy town.

Knowing what I know now, I see the humor in this story. And yes, I see the sadness, too. Luckily my family knows how much I care for and adore them, and they will not need additional therapy over this experience. As I mentioned, humility is the key to humor, and this memory is one that my family and I laugh at to this day. Even when I mentioned that I was thinking about putting it in this book, they all said, OMG, YES, you have to add that story. I think the only one in our family who doesn't know about it is my mother-in-law, so I'll be sure to tell her before the book is published.

PAUSE

Once I found myself obsessing over a tablecloth, I should have Paused!

Asking myself important questions like,

PEEL

What am I feeling? *Hot, heart racing, tightness in my chest.*

Why am I feeling this way? *I'm embarrassed, anxious, and feel ashamed.*

REVEAL

What about this situation is making me feel this way? *My mother-in-law, whom I admire and respect, doesn't think I am good enough to own a tablecloth.*

Is it true? *No.*

What is the Truth? *I don't have a tablecloth, and that makes me feel embarrassed.*

Why do I feel embarrassed? *Because I should have a tablecloth. (Notice the word "should." It's a great indicator that Ego has just entered the room.)*

Is it true? *No.*

What can I do to change it? *Accept the Truth and buy a tablecloth, or ask if she has one we could borrow.*

Winner, winner, Turkey Dinner!

HEAL

Our need to feel seen is not a one-way street. My selfishness and self-centeredness to make Thanksgiving something even Martha Stewart would be proud of trumped the people I was trying to please. Knowing this was our first Thanksgiving in our home meant they no longer had one in theirs. Her need to feel seen was in sharing, not shaming. My unsafe beliefs, however, saw it as an attack on my character and was instantly blinded by the Lies.

Putting myself in her shoes made me feel and see her for all the love she gives our family. I imagined how I would feel after decades of traditions in my home were now being passed on to my children. I would want very much to be a part of the new traditions, not their star attraction.

Had I seen the Truth and the Lie, I would have admitted that I don't have a tablecloth and would love her help in making this Thanksgiving special together. I know I am worthy and blessed. I don't have to impress anyone to know that.

As they say:

"Those that mind don't matter, and those that matter don't mind."

I chose to Eat the Banana.

It was never about the tablecloth. I got so caught up in impressing others to "feel seen" and deemed worthy that I forgot I already *was*. I already had everything that I needed. Instead, I hyper-focused on "being seen" and playing a part I never had to play.

Now there is nothing wrong with wanting to make special occasions more special by putting love and attention into the event. Even down to the cloth napkins with sparkly napkin rings that you place so elegantly on that fine China (or dixie paper plates for all I care). And trust me, my table setting is still as beautiful as it was that first Thanksgiving. The only difference is that I do it for those I love and not for them to love me. Now when we gather around that table to share a Thanksgiving meal, I feel seen as a loving wife, mother, and daughter who still cooks more than we can feed.

Progress is still progress.

15

It's Not About YOU

Although this book is mainly centered around YOU and recovery from Identity Sabotage, this chapter is slightly different. This chapter is *for* you, but it's not *about* you. Well, maybe; I guess it depends on which side of the street you're on, and that is not for me to decide.

If you find yourself on both sides of the street—and if you're being honest with yourself, you will—you'll be able to clean up the garbage that is yours and leave the rest to those it belongs to.

I wanted to cover many areas of our lives that showcase examples of how we can discover our own unsafe beliefs and stop living other people's lies as our truth. This chapter answers the question:

"Why don't some people like me?"

Do you ever wonder why some people don't like you? I'm talking about the ones that have no reason not to like you, but for whatever reason, they don't. I'm sure there are some people that don't like you for a reason, but the people we are talking about in this chapter don't have *any* reason.

Now that we have a good understanding of Identity Sabotage, I feel we are ready to tackle this question with an open mind, a loving heart, and genuine empathy for others. And if not, may the force be with you because we're diving in.

There are three main reasons why someone with no reason doesn't like you.

1. You possess something they want.
2. You represent something they lost.
3. You see them for who they really are, not the person they pretend to be.

I am not saying these are valid or fair reasons in every instance, but it's *their* reason, so get over it. (Kidding—if only it were that easy!)

As I mentioned, you may live on both sides of the street here, so take this opportunity to reflect on the people you don't like and see how your reason(s) measure up by the end of this chapter.

For your reference, and to give you a better understanding of what you're dealing with, the two main Emotional Response Types that fall into these three reasons are **Project and Redirect**.

Reason 1: You Possess Something They Want.

As we learned about Identity Sabotage, we now know that envy, jealousy, greed, and pride are fueled by the Ego. Without them, Ego would have nothing to run on. Unfortunately, there is plenty of it to go around, so Ego continues to run the show in most of our lives. (Too bad our cars don't run on Ego, even though our Ego does drive many cars... maybe that's a bad analogy, but I think you get where I was going.)

The Ugly Truth is that some people will not like you simply because you possess something they want. It doesn't have to be an expensive car in the driveway—it could be your job, family, friends, outgoing personality, looks, hair color, or even your dog.

There are countless reasons someone will not like you simply because of something you possess.

Of course, most people will never tell you their motivation and justify it by saying things that are not true to make themselves feel better for acting the way they do.

They'll say things like:

- *She is too much.*
- *She thinks she's all that.*
- *She is such a showoff.*
- *She is so stuck up.*
- *She's mean.*
- *She's fake.*
- *She's too loud.*
- *She's selfish.*

If asked why they don't like you, they honestly have no real reason based on Truth. Their sabotaged identity makes them feel *less than* you. Their warped perception allows them to see something that does not exist.

However, it is not your job to point this out to them. Well, you *could* buy them this book, flag this section, and secretly leave it on their doorstep. Totally kidding!

In all seriousness, it is not your job or responsibility to point this out or try to show them the ways of their wrongdoing. That would make you look like a narcissist, reinforcing their already distorted view of you. Just accept it, bless them, and change your view to love, only wishing for others what you want for yourself.

Reason 2: You Represent Something They Lost.

Remember, *you* are the enlightened one here and know a secret they do not. The Universe usually gives us what we need, not what we "think" we need. This is not because we are unworthy, but because we are *worthy of more*. That said, the unenlightened one may see you as a threat, competition, or the one that stole her man even though they had been broken up for more than a year. Stay in your lane here! It is crucial not to swerve to hit anyone that falls into this category. Most times, these people are hurting the deepest. We don't need to kick them when they're down. Seriously!

It becomes more obvious who these people are now that these three reasons have been presented to you.

That lady in the grocery store who always gives you the stink eye, but you've never spoken to her? You know, the one that you tried to speak to but she always turns the other way or pretends she didn't hear you? You try to find a reason why she acts this way, but you cannot come up with a single one. You begin to tell yourself stories as to why she is the way she is, which makes you feel justified in now giving *her* the cold shoulder the next time your paths cross.

Maybe, just maybe, you are now living in her old house. The one she lost due to unfortunate events. Every time she sees you, she is reminded of a dark time in her life that reopens wounds she is trying to heal.

Then there's Janice at work. You started working at your dream job and can't wait to settle in, make friends, and grow with the company. Yet day after day, Janice is distant. She won't engage in light-hearted chatter, is absent at team-building lunches involving you, and didn't even sign the "Welcome Aboard!" card you received on your first day. What did you do to make her not like you? This question races through your mind more frequently than you care to admit. You tell yourself stories to make yourself feel better that she's the Debbie Downer on the team. She's the one not to be liked, not you.

Except she *used* to have your dream job until she lost it. She was demoted for failing to meet expectations and quarterly projections. Every time she sees you, she is reminded of those reasons and beats herself up for what she has lost. You represent what she had and remind her daily of what she lost.

Then there's Tracey and her mom, Marci. Women whom you are convinced hate you. Why on Earth could these women hate you? Hate is such a strong word linked to even stronger emotions. You haven't been in the picture long enough to create reasons to justify these types of emotions. You're simply living your best life with your new husband and his daughter, who is now your stepdaughter. You've always wanted to have a family and child, and now you finally do. All you want is to enjoy this experience and love them with all your heart. You do all the beautiful things together and enjoy many family vacations and holidays, building new memories and traditions.

Sure, Tracey is the ex-wife, and Marci is the grandmother to your new stepdaughter, but you didn't cause their divorce. In fact, they had been divorced for more than 10 years before you came along. Still, their blatant rage for you fills the room whenever they are near. You begin to feel defensive and tell yourself stories about them and how pathetic they are for treating you so poorly. Feeling justified, you start to treat them poorly and follow suit.

You begin reacting to their acting; playing the victim while becoming the true villain in their story. People grieve differently and at different times. Denial plays a role in this process. Time is an illusion that we use to measure the distance between one event to the next. Ten years can feel like 10 minutes when denial is the soothing tool to heal. The

Truth was that the marriage ended due to Tracey's bad behavior, which she was now repairing. The grandmother hoped it would be enough to unite them back together. Your marriage to her ex-husband ended this delusional dream, which to them wasn't delusional at all. You now represent what once was and no longer will be.

Reason 3: You "See" Them.

The third reason is the hardest to accept and yet the most common. The desire to be "unseen." Most people will dislike you simply because you can see them, and they dislike themselves. In Chapter 14, "It's Not About the Tablecloth," I talk about *feeling seen* versus *being seen*. But there is a third way of *seeing*. When someone who wants to be *unseen* yet feels seen in your presence, they will run, avoid, and steer clear from you as if you had the latest COVID strain.

Those seeking to live life undetected hide something so big, dark, and scary that if anyone finds out, they will die. To them, the secrets they keep make them feel safe. They don't see how they are making them sicker. The more they isolate, tucking their secrets safe inside, the more comfortable they feel. Their secrets are their security blanket. You can see them; you are a threat to their security.

Most of these people are not bad people; they are sick and are not ready to take the medicine they need to heal. Therefore, the only way to protect themselves from being found out is to distance themselves from anyone who might be on to them and uncover their Truth. As I've said, it can seem easier to continue living a lie than to swallow the Truth.

These examples do not condone bad behavior. But when we see the people instead of their actions, we might find compassion and under-standing for why they behave the way they do. Our anger and resentments toward them shift to their actions, not the person.

Most people will dislike you simply because you can see them, and they dislike themselves.

STORYTIME

Applying the reasons why someone might not like me, I could see the Truth in most of them. The one area I resisted was why *I* chose not to like people. Not a big shocker considering this meant I had to get uncomfortable. What we resist persists. Our resistance to people we decide not to like are indicators that reflect what we don't like about ourselves. No wonder this part was the hardest. But as Glennon Doyle says, "We can do hard things!"

As I started to write out my list of people I did not care for, I forced myself to ask the honest question of *why*. Each name was followed with Truth, and the Truth was I was sick. I was a sick person trying to get well, not a bad person trying to be good.

Jealousy, envy, and pride took over the pages. My Ego was ruining my life.

Jealousy of people that had what I wanted; envy for not having it; and pride, well... pride is a bitch. Knowing that pride is the throne where Ego sits, it was time to sit at a different table. If I wanted to heal, I had to face my Truth and take my medicine.

No longer resisting and fighting my inner dragons, I surrendered to the people I resisted the most. Full of fear, I stepped toward faith, trusting the Universe had my back. I was willing to feel seen by people whom I knew could already see me. With vulnerability and humility by my side, I asked them for help. There were three of them!

> *When your Pride is bigger than your circumstance, you'll never advance.*

The Truth and the Lie were revealed on those pages.

Truth: *I'm not alone and never have to do it alone.*

versus

Lie: *Facing my problems could hurt me.*

I had two choices:

Eat the Banana or Die.

I chose to eat the Banana.

One was a woman I judged for being too loud, too arrogant, and too perfect. She scared me. She scared me because I knew she could see me, and allowing yourself to feel seen meant I had to reveal it all. The Truth was she had what I wanted. Even better, she had what I wanted and was willing to share it. She wanted to help me, not hurt me.

Another was a man whom I knew if I asked for help, I was going to get it. There would be no turning back, no more running. He scared me because I knew he could help me. It was only my pride that stood between us. Once I pushed pride aside, I made room for humility and Truth to step in. He provided the answers to the lessons I wasn't learning. He had solutions to the problems I couldn't solve on my own.

The third person was a woman I recoiled from like a hot flame. I immediately resisted her when I saw that she would not sign off on my

BS. What we resist persists, and she did. Everywhere I turned, there she was—the missing piece to my puzzle.

> It's funny how we pray to God to help us, yet fight the people he sends.

These three people were doing God's work in human form. They were my Shift Shapers. Joining forces with them, we formed an alliance built on reliance, not defiance. Fear was replaced with hope and shame replaced with "same," as I learned we all shared similar struggles and that my pain helped them heal just as much as theirs healed me.

I invite you to do the same. Make a list of all the people you resist. And ask yourself what unsafe beliefs they challenge. Chances are they are the answers to your prayers.

If you are not being liked, my solution is to read, understand, and accept this chapter as Truth. Please find comfort in knowing that it isn't about you. Stop beating yourself up trying to figure out what you did or what you could do to make these people like you. Stop trying to lower your vibe, dim your light, or play small. As long as you are leading with love and speaking to heal, not harm, there isn't much more you can do. Just do you and enjoy your life.

This is easier said than done when feeling under attack. My advice, however, is to not play a role in someone else's story that wasn't written for you. When we begin to play the character they have written, it's hard not to look like the villain in their story. Please don't give them material to work with. Instead, be the incredible human you are.

Be the exception, not the rule.

Rise above, not below.

Are you picking up what I'm lying down?

How many more cheesy sayings can I fit into this chapter?

I'll do us all a favor and stop here.

16

It's Not About the Destination

Have you ever heard the saying, *No matter where you go, there you are*?

I used to hate hearing it. Because it was the Truth, and the Truth was I was trying to escape "me" and wanted to believe that if I changed my environment, everything would be right with the world.

If I didn't change what was happening within ME, no matter where I showed up, I was still the same person responding to new situations with the same mindset that created the problems in my life that I was running from in the first place.

Add to that the constant desire to avoid feeling uncomfortable, less than, or unworthy, and we begin to find ourselves in this always-striving-yet-never-arriving loop.

Wherever your destination, know and own this today—

You are ALREADY there.

Once you accept this as FACT, and only until you can own this reality as Truth, can you start to receive the messages from the Universe, learn from lessons being presented to you, and grow forward.

All obstacles on our journey are there for a purpose. All bumps, road-blocks, setbacks, and challenging characters are there to help you.

Whoever says life is hard needs to read a course in miracles, take an honest look in the mirror, and re-evaluate their journey up to this point. That frustrating coworker, family member, friend, or partner is there to teach you how to be better and practice your gifts... your God-given gifts. They are opportunities to realize your power. Life doesn't have to suck; we don't have to struggle.

Sure, we will experience pain, loss, and challenging people; that is life. But we don't have to sit in the pain to learn from it. We don't need to claim it, shame it, or own it. We need to experience it, see it as a lesson, discover what that lesson is, and "grow on."

We lose sight of what we are meant to learn on the journey when we are so focused on the destination or outcome. It's all about who we are to become, or, better yet, who we are to uncover along the way. The Road Map to Enlightenment is through learning techniques that help you grow. The answers and techniques are waiting in the lessons, and the lessons are found on the journey of life, NOT the destination.

All our dreams, desires, goals, and visions of our future are already ours, just waiting to be realized. They are seeded within us deep in our souls. They are a part of our blueprint—our DNA. Those thoughts are there for a reason. However, to manifest them and physically materialize them into reality, you must acquire the skills or the keys to unlock their power.

> Disclaimer: What we perceive and what the Universe sees are not always in alignment. When we place conditions on our desires, force, control, or manipulate to receive, we are not in sync with source energy (i.e., the Universe).

I'm all for manifestation and the law of attraction, but one thing they fail to mention is that not everything we desire is meant for us. I know this sounds contradictory to what you just read above, but it's true. This is where we must let go of what we think we know and trust the process.

The Ego plays a massive role in failed manifestation. The Universe is Truth. The Ego is the Lie. The Ego tells us we need power, fame, riches, and glory to succeed. The Ego tells us we are not good enough. The Ego tells us we are unworthy. This is where the Universe and our Ego clash. The Ego tricks us into manifesting more lies when the Universe tries to deliver the Truth.

Having a spiritual connection and practice is vital to real manifestation. Through this practice, we shed our Ego Self, our False Self. We begin to let go of material dreams and awaken to our spiritual path. We pay attention to our intentions and quickly see where they are out of alignment. We place more value on self than stuff. Greed is replaced with gratitude. We begin to shift and connect to a higher frequency and disconnect from Ego.

Part of my daily practice is to pray for God's will, not mine. Before my feet hit the floor, before I drink my coffee, before I do anything else, I pray.

God (insert Higher Power, Universe, etc.)

How may I be of service today?

Help me see what I need to see, hear what I need to hear, and feel what I need to feel in order to carry out your will for me today.

Please give me the courage, strength, and power to speak, listen, and heal.

Remove any obstacles that may prevent me from fulfilling your will.

Namaste.

Before doing this daily ritual, I would start my day running on self-will. No intention to pay attention to, just my actions toward whatever it was that I thought was important. Ego was running the show, fueled by the need for instant gratification. This led to disappointment, frustration, and a reinforced unsafe belief of unworthiness. If things didn't go as I had planned them to go, I would convince myself that it was because I wasn't good enough. I wasn't worthy of receiving the things I wanted.

It was self-defeating and exhausting!

Our destiny is in the journey, and when it connects with the higher vibrations of this Universe (and it wants to connect), we start to receive messages. These messages are prompts, directions, or, better yet, reminders of why we are here! These messages are SIGNS of whom we are meant to become.

From this place, I could let go of what I thought I needed to do or become, allowing the Universe to direct my thinking. I could see where my will (Ego) was running the show and began removing the things draining my energy. The Ego loves to drain us and distract us. The more we pay attention to the external noise, the less we hear our internal Truth.

Trusting that the Universe would safely guide me, I reviewed my journey up to this point through prayer and meditation.

> *Universe, help me see where I am to go. Please show me what I am to let go of and what I am to nurture. Remove any thoughts that do not serve my purpose and Higher Good. Take away any obstacles that block this Truth and shine light where I need to see.*

Sitting quietly, I asked the Universe a question and wrote what came through as inspired thought. This is what I heard.

What am I doing? *Feeding the Ego.*

What are my intentions? *Trying to find your way.*

What are my motives? *Pure intention to help others.*

What am I trying to become? *Everyone but you.*

Who am I? *A healer.*

What is my purpose? *Heal through words, both written and spoken.*

How do I do this? *Write.*

I knew my Truth was to Speak to Heal, and although I didn't see how that would look in action, I trusted that the Universe had my back and would support me along the way. I got out of my own way and let the Universe take over.

Through my healing journey of discovery, I knew my emotional response types, I knew my primary unsafe beliefs, and I could see how my actions were feeding into my Ego. My underlying need for acceptance and people-pleasing led me down the path of healing others while it was helping heal me in the process. However, it was time to let go of the things that were no longer serving me, and it became clear what that was. I had to let go of the things draining me so I could be of service as the Universe had intended.

The Universe is here to help you manifest your Truth into reality.

> *Knowing when to let go of a dream is as important as knowing when to follow one.*
>
> *~ Jamie Kern Lima*

Be the flow and receive. I say "be" the flow instead of "go" with the flow because when we go with the flow, we take on whatever is in front of us as ours to handle. I used to "go with the flow," until I realized I was flowing down the wrong river!

I remember my dad quoting Yogi Berra many times, saying, "When you come to a fork in the road, take it." I never understood that quote until years later when I came to a fork in the river during that meditation. That fork was an opportunity to make a new decision and take the inspired path. I don't think Yogi understood just how profound his statement was.

When we are the flow, we are supported by the Universe. Energy propels us, guides us, and inspires us to act. We look forward, claim our space, and step into our power within our journey.

WE TAKE THAT FORK!!!

When we see this as our new way of being, we can finally see the beauty and purpose in our life lessons along the way. We will start to crave the process and trust in its perfection. We will begin to lean into the discomfort and know the Universe is about to deliver something magical.

My thoughts and self-will could never produce the perfect solution for what I needed in my life. Inspired thoughts, however, always delivered exactly what I needed. When I trust the Universe and do the next inspired thought, I see a path. When I doubt the Universe and do what I think the next step should be, I see a path. I have a choice to choose what path I will take—Ego or Truth. The difference between the two is that one is forced and the other is guided. And when in doubt, trust your gut and take the fork!

Here the Truth and the Lie were exposed.

Truth: *I am enough just as I am.*

versus

Lie: *I must prove myself and do more to be more.*

I had two choices:

Eat the Banana or Die.

Before then, I thought I had to be a yoga teacher, meditation guide, Ayurveda practitioner, health coach, podcast host, writer, and speaker. I believed this because I was doing this. I was doing this because I felt called to help people. I was spreading myself too thin with too many pots on the stove to attend. Some were boiling over, some were on simmer, and others I couldn't even get cooking.

I chose to eat the banana.

Once I sat and asked for inspired thought and direction, I saw this happening. I could take all my thoughts, plans, ideas, dreams, and ambitions, and compare them with my purpose to see which ones were out of alignment. I could let go of the ones that did not serve my purpose while still seeing its purpose in my life. Even though I was letting go of becoming a practicing Ayurveda consultant, the lessons I learned and the people I met gave me something I needed. The biggest being discovering my leaky gut and being given a holistic solution to heal it without medication and possibly more seizures. My yoga journey led me to many inspirational gurus that helped me heal and find my way out of the darkness I was living in. Once I removed myself from the equation, I could see why I was actually doing it and found peace in the solution.

Our path is filled with many blessings, people, and experiences, all there to help guide and support us, even though many don't even know it.

We are all on this planet at the same time for a reason. We all have a unique journey we are meant to experience and share. And it's in the sharing that we unite the pathway of our journey to **enlightenment** together.

Life isn't about winning the gold medal, having the biggest house, or having the fanciest cars. It's not about the promotions, the designer bags, and how many likes or followers you have on Instagram.

Life isn't about the destination; It's a journey of discovery and connection.

I encourage you to try my prayer and meditation from this chapter and see what you hear. Sitting quietly in a place where you will not be distracted with a pen and journal next to you, close your eyes, repeat the prayer, and listen.

> *Universe, help me see where I am to go. Please show me what I am to let go of and what I am to nurture. Remove any thoughts that do not serve my purpose and Higher Good. Take away any obstacles that block this Truth and shine light where I need to see.*

After a few minutes of sitting in the dim, ask the questions one by one, trusting your intuition.

- **What am I doing?**
- **What are my intentions?**
- **What are my motives?**
- **What am I trying to become?**
- **Who am I?**
- **What is my purpose?**
- **How do I do this?**

Write what you hear. Don't question it; just write. The answers are there if you choose to listen. Sometimes it's hard to hear the Truth, like it was for me when I heard that I was feeding my Ego. But deep down, I knew that was true. The bigger I made myself look, the more I thought people would listen and pay attention to me; the more impressive I thought I would sound or look to others. However, the reality is that when you speak from a place of love, compassion, and Truth, you don't need to force it, distort it, or manipulate it. The Truth speaks louder than any degree or designation can ever do.

So, the next time you want to change your job, relationship, or environment, take a YOU turn instead. Pause and breathe in all the goodness that surrounds you, for it is all there supporting you, guiding you, and helping you grow forward. Wherever your destination, know and own today that you are already there.

17

It's Not About the Book Deal

Who am I to write a book?

I mean, seriously, whom do I think I am? Or is it who do I think I am? I am not a writer. I was held back in fourth grade and still struggle with spelling and proper grammar. Obviously! Who am I to write a book and dare to believe it would ever be published? I even put it on my vision board that I would become a *New York Times* best-selling author. Even crazier, I wrote next to it that HAY HOUSE would be the publisher.

Never in my life did I ever think I was a writer. I didn't dare to dream such a dream because it didn't fit the narrative I was writing for myself. Yet I kept hearing this message in my meditations that I was to write. Write, write, write was all I could hear every time I sat down to meditate. For years I brushed it off as one of the delusional daydreams I used to have as a child. When I was little, I dreamed of becoming a famous actor walking the red carpet, until I was told I looked homely. I dreamed of becoming a teacher, lecturing my stuffed animals and cabbage patch dolls on the meaning of life, until I was held back. I dreamed of being an Olympic gymnast practicing my beam routine on a 2x4 in the backyard, until I was told I didn't have the right frame. In every dream I would have, the people in my life told me that I wasn't good enough.

Of course, those weren't the exact words they used, but that is exactly what I heard.

PAUSE

Knowing what I know now, why in the hell would I put myself in another situation to fail and face rejection by writing a book? The same book that led me to relapse years prior? Why do I keep setting myself up for failure and humiliation? Why can't I sit down, shut up, and live my life in gratitude for simply having one? I can't tell you how many times I have asked myself this question. Like, seriously, what is wrong with me? I have a good life today. I'm sober, I have amazing children, I have a husband who loves me unconditionally when I have given him every reason not to. I have supportive friends and more healthy relationships than I could ever imagine possible. Why isn't that enough? Why do I need to keep going to this empty wishing well, thinking that maybe my dreams will come true this time? I was content. I was at peace. Why rock the boat now?

PEEL

I have learned there is a difference between contentment and complacency, and your GUT is the compass. When you are called toward something bigger than yourself, I believe this is your intuition speaking. It is not my job to question whether or not I deem myself worthy, but when inspiration speaks, it is my responsibility to listen.

These desires kept creeping back into my dreams and meditations after every attempt to silence them because they were planted in me for a reason. The Universe will give us exactly what we NEED to grow, heal, and learn. It provides the experiences we need in order to accomplish the desired outcome it has planned. The answers are waiting in the lessons.

I began to write. Messy run-on sentences and all. I started pouring my heart onto the keyboard, one keystroke at a time. I kept writing because I trusted the lessons would reveal a deeper meaning behind my healing. I bought books about writing books. I attended multiple writing workshops and took courses on publishing a book. Hearing from every corner of the planet how subjective the publishing industry was, I just kept writing. The more I wrote, the more I learned about the uphill battle I was about to climb. Literary agents? I need a what? How do I get one of those? Query letters? Book proposals? What's that? Pitches, synopsis, bios, social platform? I'm writing a book, not running for president.

Here we go again! An underdog trying to play with the big dogs! It was clear the Universe was leading me down this path for a reason, and I was willing to find out why.

Rejection letter after rejection letter poured into my inbox.

"Your platform isn't as big as we would like to see."

"You don't have enough followers."

"This isn't for me."

"Submit to us when you have an audience worthy of our time."

The best rejection letters were the ones never sent. Not only do you pour your heart and soul into something and send it out to complete strangers in hopes they "deem" you worthy of working with them, but on average, you wait four to 12 weeks to either hear NOPE or, worse yet, nothing at all.

If the Universe was trying to teach me to stay in my lane, trust me, I was trying, but I knew that wasn't the message I was to learn. I kept writing, crafting, and perfecting my pitch. I put myself out there on social media, speaking my Truth, sharing my story, and growing my platform one follower at a time. Except they weren't just followers, they were my friends, soul sisters, and brothers. They shared a similar story and felt connected with mine. This wasn't a game of numbers; this was real life with real people! The ones I was born to write this book for.

REVEAL

Then it hit me; it wasn't about the book deal or being published by Hay House. It was about who I was becoming while writing the book and who I would be helping in the process.

So I continued writing. I didn't write for fame or glory. I didn't write to become a *New York Times* best-selling author; I wrote for me and the person reading this book. I wrote for the little girl who dared to dream. I wrote for the woman who is afraid to speak up. I wrote for my future self, who deserves to feel seen. I wrote for the underdogs who fight every day to be better than they were yesterday while the world seems to pass them by. I wrote for people struggling with addiction who feel hopeless. I wrote for everyone that felt as if they were not enough and continued to believe the lies they were told growing up. I wrote to heal.

The more I wrote, the more I connected to my Soul-Self. The more I wrote, the more I saw how life was, in fact, happening *for* me and not *to* me. The more I wrote, the more I saw that life presented me with opportunities to evolve and transform into the perfectly imperfect Human I am today. I realized that I wasn't writing as much as I was rewriting. I was rewriting the narrative I had been living as my Truth and, in return, was creating a new story that, for the first time in my life, had me playing the lead role. Instead of going with the flow, I *became* the flow. I never felt more connected to my Truth and more inspired to embrace my future.

Letting go of the false self is the most liberating feeling in the world. Shedding the old self and limiting beliefs we place on it to allow for true growth to take place is invigorating. Using the 5-Step Method again, I faced my fears of not being good enough to write a book and peeled back the lies to reveal my Truth.

The Truth was that I don't have to be an excellent speller; that's what spell check, Alexa, and editors are for. I didn't have to get excellent grades in school to become a writer; I just had to use the tools and resources provided to me and take action. I didn't have to get "published" to write a book; I just had to write. I didn't have to become a *New York Times* best-selling author to validate my message; I just had to tell it.

The less I attached my self-worth to the outcome for validation, the more relaxed and confident I became. The less I tried to "be," the more I became "me." For the first time in my life, instead of shaming and blaming myself for my past, I thanked her. I thanked her for never giving up. I thanked her for going through all the lessons she needed to learn to become the person she is today. I thanked her for her loving heart, compassion, tenacity, and grace. I thanked her for taking the hard hits and getting back up every time. I thanked her for walking into rooms where she didn't feel seen. I thanked her for her ability to forgive others and, most importantly, for her ability to forgive herself. I thanked her for not giving up on ME, for it was in her weakest moments that I found my strength.

In that strength, I found the courage to continue writing, pursuing my purpose, and creating a life I was born to live. In connecting to my Soul-Self, I finally left that corporate job that blessed me with 25 years of lessons, struggles, setbacks, and unlimited opportunities and pursued my healing practice full-time. Personally and professionally.

The more you awaken to your Truth, the harder it becomes not to live it. The more we peel back the lies and expose the Truth, the easier it will become to believe it. The fact that you are reading these words as I write them is all the proof I need and hopefully enough for you as well. Trust me, I was given every opportunity to give up and buy back into the lies my unsafe beliefs wanted me to believe. Just because things seem like they are not going in your favor doesn't mean they are not. The more my perception changed, the more I could see they were.

Outcomes are just limitations we place on ourselves. I didn't have to be an Olympic gymnast to do gymnastics. I didn't have to be a famous actress to walk the red carpet or be a teacher to teach. I didn't have to be an NFL cheerleader to dance and embrace my inner cheerleader. I didn't have to date the high school football captain, climb the corporate ladder, or have a bunch of letters after my name to prove my place on this planet. And I sure as heck didn't need to publish a book to write.

> The moment we place more worth on the process than the outcome, the sweeter the journey will be.

The Truth and the Lie were exposed.

Truth: *My worth is non-negotiable.*

versus

Lie: *My worth depends on others.*

I had two choices:

Eat the Banana or Die.

HEAL

I chose to eat the Banana and finished writing this book. Now by the time it gets to you, it will either be from a publishing house or my own house, but either way, it's now in your house. How it got there is none of my concern. My only responsibility is to enjoy the process, even if that means the only person that will read this book is me. Because at the end of it all, I am worth it!

AND SO ARE YOU!

No matter how old you are or how often you got knocked down, spit out, or tossed to the side, YOU are made from love with the "soul" purpose of being loved. It's only your unsafe beliefs that block you from the Truth.

The method is easy, but the process is messy. It exposes wounds that leave you feeling vulnerable, awakens hurts that make you feel pain, and reveals hidden Truths about yourself that may be hard to accept. But I promise you it is worth it. Having the willingness to take that first step toward spiritual enlightenment is all you need to begin. One small step leads you to the next. The Shift Shapers will be near, inspiration will become clear, and your path toward inner healing will appear.

One peel at a time!

18

It's All About the Banana Bread

By now, you should have a bunch of bananas waiting to be eaten. What better way to eat them than banana bread?

As a **THANK YOU** for reading this book to the end, I wanted to share my secret "healing bread" recipe with you.

If you're like me, you often find those bananas you intended to eat turning brown on your kitchen counter. With failed aspirations of making banana bread, we toss them into the garbage.

Instead, freeze those bananas for later and try this ritual instead.

Healing Bread Ingredients

Flour (2 cups)

Baking Soda (1 teaspoon)

Salt (1/4 teaspoon)

Butter (1/2 cup)

Brown Sugar (3/4 cup)

Eggs (2 beaten)

Bananas (3 ripe)

Healing Bread Instructions

Baking Prep:

Preheat oven to 350.

Light your favorite candle.

Play your favorite feel-good music.

Draw a warm bath.

Add 1 to 2 cups of Epson Salt.

One tablespoon carrier oil.

One drop each of Ylang-ylang, Bergamot, Myrrh.

Once your bath is drawn and all your ingredients out, combine your flour, salt, and baking soda in a bowl. (not the bath)

While mixing, repeat this Mantra.

Today I own my Truth.

I am strong.

I am courageous.

I am free.

Now for the bananas.

Each of the three bananas represents a Truth you are struggling to accept. The lie you have been living is now in your hands.

Peel back each banana while **repeating this Mantra**, putting them into a separate bowl.

I AM ENOUGH

I AM LOVED

I AM WORTHY

Once all three bananas have been peeled and placed into the bowl, begin mashing them together, repeating this Mantra.

Next, beat the brown sugar and butter in a mixer until creamy.

Add the beaten eggs.

And finally, the mashed bananas.

Add the dry ingredients to the banana mixture and mindfully combine them while envisioning fear, doubt, and worry fading away.

Pour mixture into a greased loaf pan, and place into the preheated oven for 60 minutes.

As your "healing bread" bakes, return to your bath and soak for 20 to 30 minutes.

While soaking, allow the healing properties of your bath to remove any toxic thoughts that block you from your Truth.

Breathing in Deeply and Exhaling Completely.

Relax, Recharge, Renew

Now restored and empowered, return to the kitchen, remove your healing bread, and let it cool.

While cooling, prepare some "intention" tea.

| **Recommended Teas Include** |
| Ginger |
| Chamomile |
| Lemon Balm |
| Dandelion Leaf |

Set an intention into the water before you boil it.

Hold the tea bag in your hands, setting your intentions for healing.

Once the healing bread is cooled and your tea poured,

Read aloud this affirmation.

TODAY, I stop living other people's lies and start living my Truth.

TODAY, I choose ME because I am worth the space.

TODAY, I face my fears and problems with passion and purpose to live in the solution.

TODAY, I vow to show up for ME consistently and authentically.

TODAY, I claim my dreams because I am more than a daydreamer; I am a goal-getter and giver.

TODAY, I own my NEW STORY;

I no longer let my old story own ME.

And finally,

EAT THE BANANA (bread).

Honorable Mentions

Gabriel Bernstein, for your guidance, love, and unconditional support.

Glennon Doyle, for reminding me that we can do the hard things.

Joseph Campbell, for helping me find the hero in my story "me."

Tony Robbins, for helping me break through some tough walls to write my new story.

Brene Brown, for being the best researcher/storyteller I know.

Wayne Dyer, for being my first spiritual teacher and coach from above.

LAO TZU, for leading the way and shining your light.

Maya Angelo, for being a beautiful example for humanity to follow.

Shannon Alder, for sharing your message and puncturing me where I needed healing.

Jamie Kern Lima, for getting up and suiting up every day. You are an inspiration!

Hay House, for being a source of inspiration, guidance, and a goal I will never give up on.

Books Mentioned & Must Reads

Don Miguel Ruiz's "The Four Agreements"

Masaru Emoto's "The Hidden Messages in Water"

Kate Levinson, Ph.D. "Emotional Currency"

Gabriel Bernstein, "The Universe Has Your Back"

Tonya De'laine is a woman on a mission to help others who have lost their way through addiction and other forms of *identity sabotage*, RECOVER and RISE.

Tonya is a sought-after ***Empowerment Coach*** & ***Emotional Fitness Trainer***, a certified yoga and meditation instructor, and Ayurveda Consultant.

She sees you; she understands you because she is YOU. After discovering the power of the PAUSE, she could restore her **CLARITY**, regain her voice, finally start speaking her truth, and, best yet, realize her true purpose on this planet, **HELPING** others do the same!

Her Mantra? "Speak to Heal" Through her Internationally downloaded Podcast "Soul Shack Sisters," Tonya has reached and coached thousands of women seeking clarity and purpose. In addition to her Podcast, Tonya has created Courses and Workshops centered around Identity Sabotage, written and produced Empowerment Meditations as heard on Insight Timer, and privately mentors women in her healing practice.

Empowering YOU to Live Life with Passion & Purpose.

Connect with Tonya De'laine

www.soulshacksisters.com

tiktok@yogitonya

instagram.com/soulshacksisters

twitter.com/tonya_delaine

facebook.com/thesoulshacksisters

youtube.com/soulshacksisterspodcast

Made in the USA
Coppell, TX
14 January 2023

11092310R00114